Arthur Griffiths, A. W. (Anthony William) Twyford

Records of York Castle

Fortress, Court house, and Prison

Arthur Griffiths, A. W. (Anthony William) Twyford

Records of York Castle
Fortress, Court house, and Prison

ISBN/EAN: 9783744750233

Printed in Europe, USA, Canada, Australia, Japan

Cover: Foto ©Suzi / pixelio.de

More available books at **www.hansebooks.com**

RECORDS OF YORK CASTLE

FORTRESS, COURT HOUSE, AND PRISON.

BY

A. W. TWYFORD,

Gov. H.M. Prison, York Castle;

AND

MAJOR ARTHUR GRIFFITHS,

Author of "Memorials of Millbank," &c.

WITH PHOTOGRAPHS AND WOOD ENGRAVINGS.

GRIFFITH AND FARRAN,

SUCCESSORS TO NEWBERY AND HARRIS,

WEST CORNER OF ST. PAUL'S CHURCHYARD, LONDON.

MDCCCLXXX.

THE JOINT AUTHORS OF THESE RECORDS

𝔇𝔢𝔡𝔦𝔠𝔞𝔱𝔢 𝔱𝔥𝔢 𝔅𝔬𝔬𝔨

TO

RICHARD MONCKTON MILNES, LORD HOUGHTON:

ONE OF THEM IN GRATITUDE FOR HIS

GENEROUS KINDNESS WHICH HAS EXTENDED OVER

FIVE-AND-TWENTY YEARS;

THE OTHER AS A MARK OF RESPECT FOR A NAME WHICH

STANDS SO DESERVEDLY HIGH IN THE

WORLD OF LETTERS.

CONTENTS.

CHAPTER I.
PAGE
FOUNDATION AND EARLY HISTORY 3

CHAPTER II.
SUBSEQUENT FORTUNES 25

CHAPTER III.
CASTELLANS AND GOVERNORS 63

CHAPTER IV.
EXECUTIONS AND DEATHS 89

CHAPTER V.
PRISON RECORDS 133

CHAPTER VI.
POLITICAL PRISONERS 165

CHAPTER VII.
VICTIMS OF INTOLERANCE, PERSECUTION, AND SUPERSTITION 197

CHAPTER VIII.
NOTORIOUS AND OTHER CRIMINALS . . . 235

LIST OF ILLUSTRATIONS.

	PAGE
Clifford's Tower	*Frontispiece*
View of York Minster and Castle	3
Plan of York	9
The Principal Gate	40
The "Minced Pye," or Clifford's Tower	43
The King's Manor House	81
Micklegate Bar	95
Debtors' Prison	151
Gateway at Clifford's Tower	153
Interior of an old Printing Office	164
Photograph of the first knife and fork used in York Castle prison for drawing the entrails, and quartering the bodies of persons so condemned to suffer	167
Clifford's Tower—City and Cathedral in the distance	213
The Condemned Cell in which Nevison and Turpin spent their last days	249
Execution behind York Castle in the Olden Time	273

FOUNDATION AND EARLY HISTORY.

RECORDS OF YORK CASTLE.

CHAPTER I.

FOUNDATION AND EARLY HISTORY.

THE first authentic "mention" of a Castle at York is in the reign of Athelstan. York was then the capital of Northern Britain, which Sithrick the Dane ruled. At his death in 936, his sons, Gottfried and Anlaff, in dread of conversion to Christianity, and jealous for their pagan gods, stirred up a rebellion against Athelstan, who marched northward to repress it. He fell upon his enemies so suddenly that the princes narrowly escaped capture. But they got away, one to Scotland, the other to Ireland, whence they came the following year with large armies, and again marched upon York. The king met them at Bromford, and a fierce battle ensued. Athelstan was completely victorious. He destroyed the enemy's army. Constantine, King of Scotland, was killed, twelve generals also, and five petty kings of Ireland and Wales.

After which Athelstan returned to York, and, resolved to deprive it of a focus for future rebellion, razed its Castle to the ground.

Of the origin of this Castle no trustworthy records remain. But the site was probably occupied by a fortified post even in the time of the Romans. Eboracum, or ancient York, was a place of great importance during the Roman occupation of Britain. Emperors were born and died there. It had, no doubt, its imperial palace, its temples, amphitheatre, and baths, although their position cannot now be exactly fixed, and no traces of them have been found. The Romans civilized Britain, and covered it with monuments of their magnificence; edifices of grandeur and importance were not likely to be wanting, therefore, in a city which was esteemed the capital of the north. Other Roman remains have, however, been discovered in considerable quantities. A portion of the old Roman wall and the Multangular tower are still extant; foundations of other portions of the wall and of various buildings have been laid bare, while numerous relics of Roman workmanship, such as altars, sepulchral stones, inscriptions, coffins, cinerary urns, lamps, fictile vessels, fibulæ and coins are perpetually being brought to light.[1]

A city so extensive was not likely to be left defenceless. It stood exposed, moreover, to the incursions and attacks of the turbulent northern tribes. On this account Eboracum was always a Roman military station, even from the first. It was the head-quarters of the sixth legion, which Hadrian, who considerably extended his British conquests, sent over to Britain, under the command of M. Pontius, A.D. 116. This sixth

[1] Wellbeloved: "York under the Romans," p. 47.

legion served principally in the north of England, and memorials of its residence abound in and about York. It was not employed in warlike operations alone. It constructed the Roman wall about Burdoswald and Carlisle; it worked also upon the vallum of Antoninus Pius; it contributed, no doubt, to fortify and strengthen the walls of Eboracum itself, wherein were safely lodged the wives and families of its soldiers when the legion took the field.

The stone walls of Eboracum no doubt correspond with the rampart of earth which surrounded the military camp. When the city became a permanent station, the head-quarters of a legion, the residence of the Roman Emperor or his representative the Proprætor, more solid defences than an earthwork were needed. The determination of the Roman origin of the Multangular tower, and the discovery of the Roman wall in connexion with it, plainly mark the direction of the lines of fortification. This portion coincides with the modern walls of York, and was

FOUNDATION AND EARLY HISTORY. 7

obviously designed to defend the northward approaches to the city. The defences to the eastward have not as yet been determined, but it is proved that a wall ran from Lendal the length of Coney Street, and its foundations were discovered by workmen digging to make a drain in April, 1770. These foundations were broad and massive; the cobbles composing them were so strongly cemented together, that no iron tools could separate them, and fires had to be lighted to burn out the cement. It was a triple wall, the spaces between having been filled with tempered clay close rammed. "These walls are supposed to have been built by the Romans to prevent the Ouse from overflowing that part of the city adjoining it."[2]

It seems not unlikely that they served also to continue the line of circumvallation of the city. Drake has asserted that this wall continued beyond the end of Coney Street, along Castlegate to the Fosse, terminating in the mount now

[2] Archæol. vol. ii. p. 181, quoted in Wellbeloved, p. 49.

known as Clifford's Tower, which he pronounces to be also a Roman remain. This Wellbeloved combats on the ground that there are no traces of its Roman origin, "nor have any traces of a wall been perceived since his (Drake's) time, though deep and extensive excavations have been made in that part of the city."[a]

As against this negative evidence there is the plausible argument that the Romans, who were thorough masters of the art of war, must have recognized the importance of so strong a natural position as that on which the Castle of York subsequently stood. Situated on commanding ground in an angle made by two convergent rivers, it was a point no less advantageous to defenders than it would be obnoxious to them if in an enemy's hands. The site of York Castle is indeed designed by nature as a place of arms, and is one upon which every military commander would immediately seize. There can be no question, therefore, that, whether as an integral part of

[a] Wellbeloved, p. 50.

The Castle of York as viewed from its southern aspect, as it met the eye of the Danes sailing up the Ouse, and as the site stood anno 926. The lower portion of the walls and the two flank towers have doubtless a Roman foundation. The water in front is that of the river Foss, which joins the Ouse river 250 yards below (south). The site was therefore covered on three of its four sides by water. Nothing can as yet be found to justify the belief that either the Romans, or the Normans, had a standing bridge over the river Foss, they for military reasons, probably contented themselves with a ferry bridge of boats. The ground embraced within the dotted line is modern—that which was purchased by the county, 1839, when the keep to the Castle Clifford's Tower became once more reunited to its more ancient part of the old fortress.

the walls of Eboracum, or a separate citadel or keep dominating the city, and affording a secure place of retreat if the outer lines of fortification were forced, the site of the present Castle of York was utilized by the Romans. Another cogent reason for this conclusion is that the Castle would give necessary protection to the sea-going galleys which sailed up the Ouse, and lay moored under its walls. The Ouse, in ancient times, must have contained more water than nowadays, as there is no doubt that Roman war-ships and grain-ships passed freely up the river as far as Eboracum.

Immediately opposite the Castle stands the Bail Hill, on which some ancient writers have fixed as the site of the Roman stronghold, and of the Saxon and Danish fortifications which succeeded, rather than the mound around Clifford's Tower. The probabilities are against this, however. The Romans may have built works upon the Bail as advanced posts to the Castle. Such works would have been in the nature of a *tête du pont* to cover the passage of the Ouse, and give the garrison of Eboracum a secure footing upon its right bank. If, as seems probable from its position, the Castle and lands adjoining were used also as a commissariat station or granary, then the Bail, if fortified, would have provided additional storage room within its lines. But no mention of the Bail appears until the time of William the Conqueror. As it is well-known that the Saxons and Danes generally built their Castles upon Roman sites, the conclusion is obvious, that, if a Roman fortification had stood upon the Bail, subsequent holders of York would have perpetuated the fortress. Yet there could surely have been no stronghold here when Athelstan made himself master of York, or we should have heard that he had razed it, like the Castle, to the ground. Drake's theory, therefore, that the first and original site of the Castle was the old Bayle, can hardly be accepted.

Passing from conjecture to fact, we find, in the

FOUNDATION AND EARLY HISTORY. 13

annals of Norman conquest, authentic records of the foundation of York Castle. Two years after the battle of Hastings, the north of England was still unsubdued; and William, hearing of gathering opposition, had garrisoned Durham with 700 men under the fierce Robert, Earl of Northumbria. His high-handed cruelty goading the people to madness, they rose in rebellion and slew him with all his men. The Northumbrians then marched to York and joined forces with Earl Morcar, who, with other chiefs, had resolved to oppose the Conqueror. William, however, approached so rapidly, that the Northumbrians, despairing of making head against him, submitted and were pardoned. York opened its gates, surrendered its keys, and was ostensibly received into favour. But William clearly did not trust its citizens. "To control this great city," says Freeman,[4] "William took the usual means of founding a castle. He chose a site where a high mound

[4] "Norman Conquest," vol. iv. 203.

suggests that it had been used for purposes of defence in earlier times, and which is not unlikely to have been the site of the old Danish tower of York, famous in the wars of Athelstan. (Will. Malm., ii. 134: 'Ethelstanus castium quod olim Dani in Eboraco obfirmaverunt ad solum diruit, ne esset quo se tutari perfidia posset.') It was on the peninsula ground between the Ouse and the Foss, on the mound which is now crowned by the later fortress known as Clifford's Tower, that William planted his new fortress. The position commands one main passage of the Ouse, and the waters of the Foss may, then as now, have washed the outworks of the Castle. Thus the first Castle of York arose, the Castle on the left bank of the river (Ouse), but which, distant as it was from the elder walls of Eboracum, was, then as now, held to be within the bounds of the city. (Oder. Vit., 511 c.: 'Ipse tamen, quia fidem illorum suspectam habuit, in urbe ipsâ munitionem firmavit, quam delectis militibus custodiendam tradidit.') He afterwards, as we shall see, mentions the building of the second Castle. This minute statement seems to outweigh the words of the English writers, which in strictness would imply that both of the York Castles were built at once." So Chron. Wig.: " He for swa to Eoferwia andpar worhte twezen castelas." And Florence, " Eboracum perrexit, ibique duobus castellis firmatis quingentos milites in eis posuit."

Thus Freeman quite endorses our opinion that William the Conqueror's Castle was raised upon the site of that which Athelstan destroyed. It is not said that William erected a new castle, but that he rebuilt the old. This disposes finally of any pretensions of the Bayle to be considered the original fortress of York. Freeman further tells that William appointed 500 picked knights to guard the Castle, under the command of Robert Fitz Richard, who was slain the following year, when the city rose in rebellion ; of Gilbert of Ghent, a Flemish adventurer; and of William Malet, who was appointed sheriff. The following year, 1069, William having crushed the rebellion of the north, York was a second time subdued, and this time a second yoke was added. One castle already commanded the left bank of the Ouse; another now arose on its right bank, on the mound which still bears the name of the Bail Tower, just within the later walls of the city. The navigation of the river, and with it the direct communication between the Danes of York and the Danes of Denmark, was thus brought altogether under Norman control. The new fortress, however, one which has always remained quite subordinate to the other, must have been a hasty structure of wood or of the roughest kind of masonry. For we read that it was built during the king's sojourn of eight days, and no less a person than the Earl of Hereford, the famous William Fitz Osbern, was left in command of it. Oder. Vit., 512 d.: " Rex autem dies octo in urbe morans alterum præsidium condidit, et Guillelmum Comitem Osberni filium ad custodiendum reliquit."

In September, 1069, the Danes under Osbern, brother to the King of Denmark, with whom were two sons of Harold, and the English under Earl Waltheof, were in the Humber with the avowed purpose of assailing York. The fleet ascending the river, a disembarkation was made not far from the village of Fulford, and the troops, on landing, were joined by all the Danes residing in the districts about York. The Norman chiefs, Malet and Gilbert, appear to have underestimated the enemy's forces, which comprised really the combined armies of English, Danes, and Northumbrians under the command of Waltheof, son of Siward, Earl of Northumbria, Earl Gospatrick, and several principal Thegns. Yet Malet looked for a siege, and, to clear the ground about his fortifications, set fire to several houses in the suburbs. But the conflagration spread so rapidly that a great part of the city was burnt down, including the Minster of St. Peter, and with it a valuable library, the gift of Archbishop Egbert in the year 800. The assailants reached York while the fire still raged, and, under cover of it, approached the walls. Dividing their forces into two columns, they stormed the two strongholds, and carried them by escalade. The Normans were all cut to pieces; of 3000 men none escaped but Gilbert of Ghent and the High Sheriff Malet with his wife and two children, and a few others.

William the Conqueror was not disposed to submit tamely to the loss of York. He soon made his appearance before the city, and, with terrible menaces, summoned it to surrender. Waltheof, who had been appointed governor, stoutly refused, and a lengthy siege began. Possibly the gallant defenders of York might have succeeded in beating off the Conqueror's attack had not William astutely bribed the Danes to withdraw and leave the garrison to fight single-handed. Even then attempts to carry the place by storm signally failed, and William of Malmesbury describes how Waltheof stood singly in the breach and cut down all the Normans who endeavoured to enter it. But famine triumphed where direct assault had failed. The garrison was at length compelled to capitulate, on favourable terms, which William quite disregarded, and put every soldier, Englishman and Scot, to the sword. After that he destroyed the city, and laid the whole district waste.

How thoroughly this barbarous measure was accomplished is fully described in the chronicles of the time. Every living thing was killed. Desolation reigned on every side.

"William turned again, and held what he had sworn,
All mad he wasteyn Pasture Medow Korne.
And slough both Fader and Sonne, women lete their gon,
Hors and Houndes their ete uncithis skaped non." [5]

Odericus Vitalis, a Norman monkish chronicler of the time, cannot exonerate his fellow-countryman William: " Nusquam tanta crudelitate usus est Gulielmus hic turpiter vitio sucubuit,

[5] Old Rhyme in Peter Langstaff's Chronicle.

durus iram suam regere contempsit et reos innocuos que pari animadversione peremit." Such was the distress, so widespread the devastation, that no less than one hundred thousand people perished upon this occasion.

For nine years following, neither plough nor spade were put into the ground. "Many of the wretched inhabitants who had escaped slaughter were reduced to the necessity of eating dogs, cats, and even their own species."[6] There was not one inhabited house between York and Durham; their deserted streets were lurking-places for robbers and wild beasts. All Yorkshire was a wilderness. Dead bodies lay scattered about in every direction; those who still lived, and had escaped fire, hunger, or the sword, fled from the land.

When the work of devastation was complete, William returned to spend Christmas at York. During his absence, his troops and workmen had been busily employed in repairing the

[6] Hargrove, i. 68.

Castles, and William, having inspected them and satisfied himself of their strength, moved westward to Chester.

It was probably on this occasion that one of the Cliffords was made constable or governor of the fortress. Who he was exactly has not come down to us, but the family was by this time established in the north, and, endowed with wealth and wide possessions, destined to take a prominent part in the stirring history of these eventful times.

SUBSEQUENT FORTUNES.

CHAPTER II.

SUBSEQUENT FORTUNES.

No particular mention is made of York Castle in the reigns immediately following the Conqueror's. It is stated, incidentally, that William Rufus strengthened its fortifications still further, and no doubt, as the central stronghold of the principal city of the north, the Castle was always closely and carefully held. It was not until the time of Richard that Castle and Tower became notorious as the scene of a brutal massacre of Jews. Full and authentic details of this bloodthirsty and disgraceful episode have come down to us.

William the Conqueror, shrewd and far-seeing statesman, had first introduced the Jews—at that time a generally proscribed race—into

England. He no doubt realized the advantage of protecting a people who then as now were the accredited bankers of sovereigns and states. A tribe or section of Jews had established themselves in York, and thriven rapidly. The place was clearly one of considerable trade; it communicated by the Ouse and Humber direct with the sea, and there is evidence to show that shipping, numerous and of considerable tonnage, frequented it from beyond the seas. Besides the profits of legitimate commerce, the Jews followed their usual profitable occupation of money-lending, earning wealth thereby, of course, but also the hatred of needy Norman baron and roystering squire, whom they bled and befriended at one and the same time. The sense of obligations received did not mitigate those feelings of loathing which the Hebrew race at that time almost universally inspired. On the contrary, Christians who were deeply indebted to them found their intolerance whetted, while others of an avaricious nature looked upon the Jews as their natural prey. These unhappy aliens were therefore constantly plundered by prince and people alike, and, in spite of rich presents offered in propitiation to the reigning powers, were never entirely safe from oppression.

Richard I., whether from pure hatred or from reasons which do not appear, had expressly ordered that the Jews should not be present at his coronation. They were prohibited from appearing in church or at the banquet. Many leading Jews nevertheless flocked to London, summoned thither to join in the presentation of some rich gift to the new king, intended to secure for them the confirmation of their liberties and privileges. Among others came Benedict and Jocenus, two wealthy Jews of York, and the chroniclers describe their pompous retinue and the display they made. In spite of the king's edict, several Jews mixed with the crowd on the day of coronation. They were detected, beaten, and abused, and some were slain. Then the people of London, eager for plunder, rose and commenced a general massacre, wherein many Jews, with their wives and children, were killed, while their houses were sacked and given to the flames. Severe measures taken by Richard repressed these excesses; but, although checked in London, the contagion had spread to other cities, and the example of the capital was promptly followed by Norwich, Lynn, Stamford, and especially by York.

Benedict and Jocenus had both mixed in the coronation throng. Upon the former, who was badly bruised in the struggle, forcible hands were laid, and he was dragged to a church hard by, and baptized against his will. He boldly spoke up for the faith of his fathers when brought next day before the king, declaring that he had been forced into baptism, but remained a Jew in his heart, and should ever do so. He now craved death as better than his late bad usage, whereupon he was driven from the king's presence, restored to his own people, and soon afterwards expired. Jocenus returned to York, and met a more terrible fate.

For a time the animosity against the Jews in this city slumbered; but, upon the king's departure for Palestine, a conspiracy was formed against them, which waited only favourable opportunity to burst forth. One night a part of the town took fire, and while many were busy extinguishing the flames, a band of evil doers broke into the house of the deceased Benedict, and pillaged it. Benedict's family were all massacred, the house was gutted and destroyed. Alarm spread among the Jews. Many of them feared a similar fate, Jocenus especially. Dreading the fury of the mob, he obtained permission to remove with all his belongings and vast wealth into the Castle, which was the king's, and should afford him protection. Nor did he retire too soon to a place of safety. A few nights later, his house also was attacked, but found empty; after which the Jews generally withdrew with their families, and all their goods and chattels, to this same sanctuary of the Castle. Here they might have remained in safety until the fury of the storm was spent, but unhappily thèy behaved with a foolish indiscretion, which had the most fatal consequences for all.

The governor of the Castle (whose name has not been discovered) having occasion to leave the Castle, as the chroniclers describe it, although more probably it was the Tower, " when he would have returned he was prevented by the Jews, who feared lest in this time he might have made some agreement with their enemies to deliver them up." The governor appealed forthwith to the high sheriff,[1] who became "angry to the last degree, which was still more inflamed by those near him who wished the Jews no good by saying that it was the highest indignity to the person of the king himself to have one of the most considerable fortresses in the kingdom seized by these miscreants." The

[1] Randal de Glanville.

sheriff thereupon by writ ordered out the Posse Comitatus to besiege the Castle. " Now," says Hemingford, " was shown the zeal of the Christian populace; for an innumerable company of armed men, as well from the city as country, rose at once and begirt the fortress round." The besieging force was so numerous that the high sheriff could not control it, and, fearing excesses, he began to regret that he had summoned the people to his aid. The better classes had held aloof, but there were many of the clergy in the crowd, notably a friar of the Præmonstratensian order, who, habited in a white vesture, busied himself by encouraging the assailants in a loud voice, till, venturing too near the wall, he was brained by a large stone let drop from the Tower.

The Jews in their extremity, dreading the worst, offered a large sum as ransom, which was peremptorily refused. Meu, a foreign rabbi, who had come to England to teach and instruct the English Jews, stood up and strongly urged them to die for their law, by their own or one another's hands, rather than fall into those of their enemies. Some faint hearted rejected this terrible counsel, but not so the rest. Those who were resolved to die, having first broken up and injured their effects in gold, silver, and rich stuffs, set fire to the towers of the Castle, "whilst their companions who had chosen life looked sullenly on, each man prepared for the slaughter. Being told by their elder that those who bore the steadiest minds should first cut the throats of their wives and children, the celebrated Jocenus began the execution by doing that barbarous act on his own wife Anna and five children. The example was speedily followed by the rest of the masters of families; and afterwards the rabbi cut the throat of Jocenus himself, as a point of honour he chose to do him above the rest. In short, the whole crew of miserable men, who had thus voluntarily given themselves up to destruction, slew themselves or one another, and amongst the rest fell their impious adviser."[2]

The remnant still alive unable to check the conflagration in the Castle, described next day to the besiegers what had occurred, and, when these were incredulous, threw many dead bodies of their brethren over the walls. They begged hard for mercy, promising all of them to become Christians, to which terms the besiegers seemed to agree till admitted within the Castle, when, under a ringleader surnamed Mala Bestia from his brutality, a general massacre took place. Great numbers of dead bodies were thrown down the Castle well. This, when sounded in 1879, was only twelve feet deep. No doubt quantities of earth had been thrown upon the corpses, and other sweepings and rubbish must since have accumulated in the place. After the recovery of the Castle, a rush was made to the Cathedral, where was deposited in great coffers the bonds the Jews held of so

[2] Roger of Hovenden and Mathew de Paris.

many Christian debtors. These were extracted and publicly burnt, to the great satisfaction of all. In this massacre some 1500 men, women, and children, all told, were destroyed. This terrible massacre was in some respects the prototype of the awful tragedy enacted in 1857 at Cawnpore.

Ancient writers, in using the word Castle, would seem to imply that it was the whole stronghold which the Jews seized. This view is supported by the statement that all the towers of the Castle were set on fire. But the garrison of the Castle must surely have been numerically stronger than the Jews, or the Governor would hardly have given them protection. Nor could the Jews have seized the Castle without the keep. The troops in the keep, or Clifford's Tower, would have looked down upon and commanded the Castle. What seems most probable is that the Jews were interned for greater security in the keep itself, which, detached and separated from the main castle by its own moat, with its own drawbridge and sallyports, might easily have been seized and held against the Governor.

Richard is reported to have called his bigoted and ruthless people to serious account for their brutal treatment of the Jews. Being absent from the realm, he desired the Bishop of Ely, his chancellor and regent, to go down in person to York, and punish all offenders without favour or affection. The chief culprits fled, and the punishment took the shape of a heavy fine upon the city. Hemingford says, "the Bishop rather sought to satisfy his own avaricious temper by mulcts, fines, &c., than do the justice he ought to have done; for not one man either then or since was executed for his villainy."

The names of two places in and about the city still testify to the sojourn of the Jews. One is Jubbergate or Jewbargate, the other Jewbury or Jewborough.

In the centuries following, York was often enough the centre of stirring scenes; the tide of civil war ebbed and flowed around it; kings summoned hither the burgesses of the kingdom to meet in Parliament assembled; the city saw now the pageantry of a mediæval court, and now was encircled with a beleaguering host, and all its echoes were loud with the din of battle and of siege. But through it all the Castle remained in the hands of the king and of the lieutenants who held it for him. It was the official residence of the high sheriffs during their term of office. Several accounts are to be met with in the Pipe Rolls which the high sheriff gave in from time to time for the repairs of the Castle. The accounts were paid by the Crown. So long as it thus remained in the king's hands, the Castle served as a store-house and magazine for his revenues of the north, just as in the times of the Romans. A constable of the Castle was appointed to have all such stores in charge, as appears from the statement of Sir Thomas Widdrington, that mention is made in an assize of Henry III. of the fees and customs belonging to the office of constable. Again, by the 13th Richard II. cap. 16, it is enacted that the king's castles which are severed from the counties shall be rejoined to them: "from whence it is supposed the assizes of the county of York were always held in the Castle, which hath reference to all the three Ridings of the county, but yet stands in none of them; neither is it within the liberties of the city, though it be always assessed, and bears charges with the parish of St. Mary Castlegate."[3]

Falling into decay, the Castle was again rebuilt or repaired in the reign of Richard III. But Leland found it in a very ruinous condition. "The area of this," he says in his Itinerary, vol. 5, "is no very grete quantitie; there be five ruinous towers in it." "The arx is al in ruine, and the foote (foot or base) of the hille that it standeth on is environed with an arme derived out of Fosse water." He describes Clifford's Tower as also in a dilapidated condition. Why thus

[3] Hist. of City of York, (1785) ii. 294.

neglected does not appear; but that it was intended to be defended at all costs is evident from the grant of lands adjoining to be holden by special tenures relating to the custody and safeguard of the Castle. Thus Robert Balistairus and John de Watringham held "by sergeantry" certain acres on condition of providing a "balister" for the defence of the Castle. Agnes de Givendale held one messuage and land in East Givendale to find one Ballister in a certain tower in the Castle of York for the safe custody of the Castle for forty days in time of war. Others were bound to find the services of an archer, or of a man with bow and arrows, whenever required. This probably was not often, as the Castle was seldom actually menaced, being far within the *enceinte* of the city walls. So it gradually fell into ruins, till the sharp struggle commenced between King Charles and his Parliament. Charles had paid several visits to York when bound northward to repress the rebellion of the Scots; and later, when his troubles were gathering thick around him, he long made the cathedral city his court and head-quarters. The necessity for restoring the fortifications of the city of York now became paramount, and the Castle "was looked upon as proper for the purpose. By the direction of Henry, then Earl of Cumberland, Lord-Lieutenant of the northern parts and Governor of York, this tower was repaired; a considerable additional square building put to it on that side next the Castle, on which, over the gate in stone work are placed the royal arms and those of the Cliffords, viz., chequée and a fess ensigned with an earl's coronet supported by two wiverns with this motto, *Désormais.*" These arms are still (1879) to be seen over the gateway.

Clifford's Tower was repaired and strengthened, a drawbridge and "pallisadoes" were added, the moat was deepened, a platform was placed upon the top, which mounted two "demi culverins" and a "saker," the heavy cannons of an age when eighty-one ton guns were as yet unknown. Colonel Sir Francis Cob was appointed Governor of the Tower and Castle, and he "with his Lieutenant-Colonel, Major, and

The principal gate or entrance was from the court on the east side, near "Castle Mills;" and there was a smaller one, as above, from the city, on the north side. (Hargrove, 1818.) Twelve years before the moat on this north side of the Castle was filled up, and a wall was built, surmounted with iron palisades, in lieu of it.

Captains, had his lodgings there during the siege of 1644. Sir Thomas Glemham, who held York for the king in that siege, made a stout and prolonged stand, but, overborne by numbers and without supplies, he was compelled to come to terms. These, as recorded, were highly favourable to the people of York, guaranteeing them their rights and privileges, and promising that, if any garrison be placed in the city, 'two parts in three shall be Yorkshire men;' the Royalist troops were suffered to march out with their arms, with drums beating and colours flying, match lighted, bullet in mouth, bag and baggage." Many changes were made, however, in the corporation; a new lord mayor and several new aldermen were appointed, all noted for their disaffection to the king. The city walls were put in repair, and the place held as heretofore, till the execution of the king and the submission of the north allowed the Parliament to "dismantle the city of its garrison," which was accordingly done, "Clifford's Tower only excepted, of which the Lord Mayor, one Thomas Dickenson, was appointed Governor, and so continued for several years."

The charge of the keep is said to have remained in the hands of the mayors of York until the appointment of Lord Frescheville at the time of the restoration. Sir John Reresby succeeded in 1682, after waiting twenty years for his predecessor's shoes. In his memoirs, which give so much information concerning those times, he says, "It was not till October, 1682, that the question of bringing the river about the Tower was considered;" probably the original moat had become silted up. The moat may have run round the Tower extending from the river Foss to the west end of the Castle wall, returning round the Tower to the river, but it is more likely that it only ran from the river Foss to the west end of the Castle wall, thus separating the Citadel from the Castle, communication being maintained by the drawbridge already mentioned.

Sir John Reresby's governorship was made memorable by the explosion in Clifford's Tower, which rendered it ever after uninhabitable. The Tower was thus blown up on the night of the 23rd April, 1684:—"About ten o'clock," says an old manuscript diary of those times quoted by Hargrove,[4] "happened a most dreadful fire within the Tower called Clifford's Tower, which consumed to ashes all the interior thereof, leaving standing only the outshell of the walls of the

Prior to the "Minced Pye" being blown up, its appearance was as represented in the above engraving. A very old tradition of the Clifford family says, "Whilst Clifford's Tower stands in York, that family will never be forgotten." The anagram of the first Earl was—"Georgius Cliffordius, Cumberlandius, dorides regno clarus cum di fulgabio." The woodcut is Hargrove's, 1818.

Tower, without other harm to the city save one man slain by the fall of a piece of timber blown up by the force of the flames, or rather by some powder therein. It was generally thought a wilful act, the soldiers not suffering the citizens

[4] ii. 252.

to enter it till too late; and what made it more suspicious was that the gunner had got out all his goods before it was discovered." Hargrove goes on to say that there is little doubt the Tower was intentionally destroyed. The soldiers had removed all their property beforehand. It is also probable that the citizens had a hand in the plot, if they did not actually originate it. The Tower dominated the city, and was so irksome to the citizens that it was a common toast in the city to drink to the demolition of the "minced pie." The Tower was so nicknamed from its appearance.

James II. seems to have turned an honest penny by selling the ruins of the keep with several other lands in and about the city to Messrs. Babington and Driffield, who held it by grant from him. From which time it remained as private property until, in 1829-34, it with other adjacent lands was purchased by the county for the purpose of enlarging the Castle of York prison, rendering the same more secure, and the whole was enclosed by the massive walls as now standing, 1879. Excepting the Tower, that portion of land on which the present male criminal prison stands, and that portion extending from the outer gates by the road to the Governor's house, all the land including the green was enclosed within the walls of the Castle, rebuilt by William I., and handed over to the care of the county, 1377-99.

During the reign of Henry III., 1216-72, the king's Castle was used for all classes of persons. Peers and peasants, debtors and felons, found themselves within its walls. On the transfer of the Castle to the care of the county, its towers were still used as prisons, until, in 1701, they had become so ruinous, and the gaol they constituted was deemed so miserable, even in those days of callous indifference to prison requirements, that they were dismantled and wholly pulled down. The new gaol (now the debtors' prison) was considered, and justly, "a most magnificent structure." It was certainly more spacious than most then existing in the kingdom. The erection of the whole pile was carried out by a tax of 3d. in the pound upon all lands in the county, pursuant to an Act of Parliament obtained for the purpose. The greater portion of the stone used appears to have been taken from the ruins of the Abbey of St. Mary's. The king, in 1701, under his sign manual, gave licence to pull down and carry away so many of the stones belonging to the manor of St. Mary's Abbey as should be set out and approved of by Sir William Robinson and Robert Byerley towards the rebuilding of the county gaol.

This gaol was, however, the same as that which Howard found when making his celebrated visitation of the prisons of England, and he does not speak in language of unqualified admiration of York Castle, although the prison was undoubtedly above the average of the time. The great philanthropist, describing York Castle, says, " In the spacious area is a noble prison for debtors, which does honour to the county.

You ascend by a fine flight of stone steps to a floor on which are eleven rooms, full sixteen feet square, and near twelve feet high. Above them is the same number of rooms, one of two of those for common-side debtors. The rooms are airy and healthy. On the ground-floor are the gaolers' apartments, &c. The felons' courtyard is down five steps; it is too small and has no water; the pump is just outside the palisades. The day-room for men is only twenty-six feet by eight; in it are three cells; in another place nine cells, and three in another. The cells are in general about seven feet and a half by six and a half, and eight and a half high, close and dark, having only either a hole above the door about four inches by eight, or some perforations in the door of about an inch in diameter; not any of them to the open air, but into passages or entries. In most of these cells three prisoners are locked up at night, in winter for fourteen to sixteen hours; straw on the stone floors; no bedsteads.

"There are four condemned rooms about seven feet square. A sewer in one of the passages often makes these parts of the gaol very offensive, and I cannot say they are clean. Indeed, a clean prison is scarcely ever seen, where the water is to be brought in by the gaolers' servants.

"Women felons are kept quite separate; they have two courtyards, but no water; you go down four steps to their two rooms—a day-room and a night-room. Their condemned cell is in another part of the gaol; near it is a room to confine debtors who do not behave well.

"The county pays one John Sherwood £10 a year to inspect and weigh the bread and deliver it to the prisoners.

"There is a grand Shire Hall in the Castle yard, almost finished. I hope the gentlemen of this great county will not stop there, but proceed to build a proper prison for felons, in which boys may be separated from old offenders, and the other inconveniences of the present gaol avoided."[5]

---

[5] Howard, State of Prisons, i. 398.

SUBSEQUENT FORTUNES. 49

The Basilica or Town Hall, to which Howard refers, was built at the expense of the county, and opened in 1777. It is the well-known Assize Courts still standing, and may still be characterized, as it was when new, as " a superb building of the Ionic order, 150 feet in length, and 45 feet in breadth. . . . . The entrance is by a loggio of six columns, 30 feet in height, over which are placed the king's arms, an elegant statue of Justice, and other emblematical figures."

The same authority goes on to say that, " At a meeting of the Justices of the three Ridings, holden on the 4th May, 1779, plans and elevations of a building to contain many conveniences much wanted at the Castle were approved of. The front of the building to be opposite and similar to the middle part of the new Courts of Justice, and the inside to contain rooms for the Records and Clerk of Indictments, rooms for petty offenders, debtors, &c., a women's apartment, and hospital rooms."

This building was erected in the following year, but considerable additions were made to it in the year 1803, under the direction of Mr. Atkinson, architect. It was one hundred and fifty feet in length, and contained the rooms and offices already specified, behind which "there is a day-room twenty-four feet by fifteen, for prisoners charged with misdemeanours. In it is a fireplace with benches, &c.; and the room is well lighted, and opens into a court-yard forty feet wide by twenty-four in depth. There are also four sleeping-cells on the ground floor of this wing. The first and second stories of it have each a day-room, with sleeping-cells and other accommodations."[6]

This building is now the female prison, but great alterations have been made in it in passing years. All the upper part has been reconstituted into separate cells for female prisoners; the present chapel also occupies the back part of the building.

[6] Hargrove, ii. 242.

One or two points of interest remain to be touched upon relative to the jurisdiction of authorities, and the limits of their boundaries in and about the Castle.

A belief has long existed that the right to use the Prison Green for public purposes, as for General Elections for the county, was a right granted by ancient charter; but so long as the Castle was a military post, it could scarcely have been possible to admit the public indiscriminately. In the absence of precise information, the conjecture seems probable that the custom was originated at the time the Castle was handed over to the county, and when two members were returned to Parliament by the whole county of York. Since the Ridings have returned their own members, their election has not taken place in the Castle, nor have the Green and the Assize Courts been used as polling-places.

The writer of the History of York, 1785, relates, "that at the distance of about seventy-seven feet from the entrance to the Castle (by Castlegate) are erected the city arms, as the extent of their liberties; here the City Sheriffs stand (as now, 1879) to receive the Judges of Assize and to conduct them to the Common Hall (the City Courts)." It was not for nothing that this landmark was erected, for the Sheriffs of the County have often laid claim to that part of the street called Castle Hill, and have made arrests thereon: notably in 1472, when the then Lord Mayor was horrified to hear that the County High Sheriff had caused to be arrested on the Castle Hill (the approach in Castlegate Street within the contested limit) one Agnes Ferrand, commonly known to be the concubine of the Rector of Wath, and had carried her prisoner to the Castle.

Drake goes on to say, " The Mayor, much grieved at this presumption, sent messengers to the High Sheriff to acquaint him that he had done contrary to the liberties and privileges of the city in arresting Agnes in the said place, and required him to deliver her up. The High Sheriff answered preremptorily that he would not, but would detain the prisoner till he had certified King and Council of the fact. However, as the record adds, Sir William Harrington, lately High Sheriff, an honourable person and a friend to both parties, hearing of it, being then in the Castle, sent the Mayor that if he would come down on the morrow to the monastery of the Augustine Friars, he would bring them together, and try to make a good end of this matter. At this meeting the whole affair was talked over betwixt them, the result of which was the High Sheriff gave up the lady, and commanded her to be conveyed to the place from whence she had been taken."

As the Castle of York was always from the first closely connected with the administration of justice, a few notes as to earlier legal functionaries and curious occurrences may not be deemed irrelevant here.

Anciently the civil government of the county

was lodged in the earl or count, to whom it was committed by the king, at will, sometimes for life, and afterwards in fee (feoffee). He was followed by the Shire-reeve, i.e. Governor of the shire or county, who before the 9th of Edward II. was elected by the freeholders. Afterwards the appointment was made by the king. His office was to execute the king's writs, return juries, and keep the peace; and his jurisdiction was called a Baili-wick, because he was the Bailiff of the Crown Shire-reeve—sheriff.

The first High Sheriff of York was W. Malet, 3rd of William I. In the time of Henry VIII., Lord-Lieutenants of shires and counties were first appointed, as extraordinary magistrates, constituted only in times of difficulty and danger.[7] Sheriffs held courts for inquiry into all criminal offences against the common law; the County Court was to hear all civil causes under forty shillings, and the Court of Common Pleas to determine any case whatever, cognizable in a court of common law, 1776.

[7] Manning and Bray's Surrey, vol. i. p. 25.

Exactly a century after the battle of Hastings, a judicial system was promulgated in the "Assize of Clarendon." In this document occurs the first mention of a body which, so far as criminal matters are concerned, can be directly compared with the juries of modern times. This and the laws of the Conqueror afford the connecting links between the fellow-swearers of old and the jurors of to-day. According to the Assizes, inquiry was to be made respecting murder, robbery, and theft, by means of the oaths of twelve lawful (free, not outlawed) men of every hundred, and four lawful men of every village, in every county in the realm. Any one charged before the justices or before the sheriffs, either as principal or as accessory, was to be apprehended and tried by the ordeal of water. The nearest approach to this scheme before the Conquest is to be found in the laws of King Ethelred, which, however, refer only to the northern part of England. It is there provided that in every wapentake, the Reeve and the twelve elder and superior Thanes shall swear to accuse none who are innocent, and to conceal none who are guilty. By the law of William I., "It is provided that a person accused in the hundred by four is to clear himself by the hand of twelve." Hand upon holy things were the twelve Thanes to place when they swore; hand upon holy things was the rule whenever oath was made. Twelve is a number which, before the Conquest, appears only as an exception in the northern shires. Immediately after the Conquest it is the favourite number in the selection of bodies which have to give a verdict of any kind. Circuits of barristers were first established in the time of Henry II., from which date also Grand Juries, as now existing. But the reader is referred for details, beyond the scope of this book, to Owen Pike's most interesting "History of Crime in England," who says, "It has been denied that the use of torture was known to the English law. That it was known, however, is certain, though it was not legally permitted, except by licence of the

King or Council. In one form, too, it could be applied by order of a Judge; not, indeed, to extract evidence, but to make a mute prisoner plead, or to punish him for not pleading. Having been warned, he received the

'JUDGMENT OF PENANCE.'

' That you be taken back to the prison whence you came, to a low dungeon into which no light can enter; that you be laid on your back on the bare floor, with a cloth round your loins, but elsewhere naked; that there be set upon your body a weight of iron as great as you can bear —and greater; that you have no sustenance save, on the first day, three morsels of the coarsest bread, on the second day three draughts of stagnant water from the pool nearest to the prison door, on the third day again three morsels of bread as before, and such bread and such water alternately from day to day until you die.' "

Standing mute was not held equivalent to

conviction. Many suffered this terrible form of death to save their estates for their children, which would have been forfeited otherwise.

Chief Justice Fortescue preferred theft with violence to theft without. "More men," he says, "were hanged in England in one year for robbery or manslaughter than in France in seven, because the English had better hearts;" the Scotchmen, also, did not dare to rob, they only committed petty larcenies. Not the least important indeed of the powers acquired by the private landholder before the Conquest was that of private jurisdiction. Little is known of its history before that time. But the technical terms which the conquerors were compelled to adopt, which belong to the language of the vanquished, and which remain untranslated in the Latin treatises of the Norman lawyers, give sufficient evidence of the institution. The gallows (*galga*) for hanging men, and the pit for drowning or half-drowning women, were among the most cherished appurtenances of the manor, or of its prototype as it existed, and in the abbey thereafter, before 1066.

The Manor Court (Mayor's Court) is a memorial of a time when a baron possessed a prison into which he could throw "hand-having" or "back-bearing" thieves, before he hanged them. With the attempt to render the ancient system of police effective was combined a change in the method of administering justice. After Magna Charta the Justices in Eyre continued their circuits, but in the reign of Edward I. the commissions by virtue of which they sat were more clearly defined. The distinction between the Commissions of Nisi-prius or Assize and that of Oyer and Terminer was well marked, and Judges of Assizes became also Judges of Gaol Delivery. In the first year of the reign of Edward III. good and lawful men of each county were appointed to keep the peace, and the present Justice of the Peace is the fully-developed evidence of those ancient guardians, who were appointed owing to England being in a state of brigandage. (See Pike, vol. i. p. 222.)

In the confusion which followed upon the abolition of the "ordeal," the judges seem to have been thrown into some perplexity by the refusal of prisoners to submit themselves to any kind of trial. In the reign of John an accused person who went to the "fire and water," and failed to clear himself, was hanged. Two years after these tests had ceased to be applied in England, some criminals made the experiment of standing mute on trial, and their fate was precisely what it would have been had they been convicted by the "Judgment of God." Early in the reign of Edward I. a number of malefactors were surrounded and attacked by the Sheriff of York. Some were killed, some made prisoners, some beheaded on the spot, because they would not consent to be tried according to the law and custom of the realm.

CASTELLANS AND GOVERNORS.

CHAPTER III.

CASTELLANS AND GOVERNORS.

AT the time of the Norman Conquest, Earl Morcar was Governor of York and all its fortresses. William did not at first displace him, being too busily engaged to attend to affairs so far north. But when Morcar and his brother Edwin, Earl of Chester, set themselves up against the Norman yoke, William hastened northward with considerable forces, and took possession of York, where he built the Castle as already described. Morcar had fled to Scotland, and his place as Governor of York was filled by William Malet, a faithful adherent of the Conqueror, who had come over with him and had been present at the battle of Hastings. Malet was constituted High Sheriff of Yorkshire, but his residence was within the Castle, where he narrowly escaped from the massacre of the garrison when York was attacked and captured by the Saxons and Danes. Waltheof was Governor during its tenure by these insurgents against William. After its recovery by the Normans, William appointed William Fitz Osbern to hold York, but it was probably about this time that the Cliffords first came to be connected with the Castle. One of the Clifford family, says the historian of York, was made the first Governor of the Tower which still bears the name of Clifford. " Sir Thomas Widdrington says," continues our author, " from the authority of Walter Strickland of Boynton, Esq., whom he calls an excellent antiquary, that the Lords Clifford have very antiently been called Castelyns, wardens, or keepers of this Tower. But whether it be from hence that the family claim the right of carrying the city's sword before the king in York we know not."[1]

[1] Hist. of York, i. 302.

Later a contention arose upon this point which may be referred to here. When James I. was approaching York on his march from Scotland southward, to be crowned at London, a gentleman of Lord Clifford's (Earl of Cumberland) household came to the Lord Mayor and Corporation, to claim his lord's right to bear the city's sword before the king. This they would by no means finally allow, but were content to abide by the king's decision. "The Lord Mayor would deliver the sword to the king himself, and leave it to his pleasure who shall bear the same, whether the Lord Mayor, Earl, or any other." It appeared, then, that while the Earl of Cumberland claimed the right of inheritance, Lord Burleigh did so also, as Lord President of the Council established in the northern parts. Upon which the king, by Sir Thomas Chaloner, sent to the Lord Mayor of York his decision. He gave it in favour of the representative of the Cliffords, saying "that the Earl of Cumberland had oftentimes affirmed, in the time of Queen Elizabeth, that he ought and had the right to carry the sword before the Queen if she came to the City of York, and that his ancestors had borne the same before other her progenitors, Kings of England, within this city, and that it was his inheritance; and the common report of the antient citizens is, and of long time had been, that it belonged to the said Earl." Some demur was, however, made when Lord Clifford, the Earl of Cumberland's son, in the reign of Henry VIII., claimed the right in his father's absence. Honourable persons in favour with the king alleged that "howbeit the Earl of Cumberland had such right, yet his son, the Lord Clifford, could have no title thereunto in the life of his father, and they also objected that the Lord Clifford rode on a gelding furnished on the northern fashion, which was not comely for that place." The son, however, stoutly maintained that " the Earl, his father, being employed in the King's affairs, he trusted that his absence should not be made use of to the prejudice of his inheritance; and for the supply of his the defects of his horse and furniture, Sir Francis Knolls, a pensioner, alighted from his horse and gave him to the Lord Clifford; and King Henry VIII., perceiving the Earl's right, dispensed with his absence and delivered the sword to the Lord Clifford, his son, who carried it before the King within the city."

When James, fourteen years later, came again to York in his progress to Scotland, another question was raised. The Chamberlain then requested Sir Francis Clifford, Earl of Cumberland, to carry the king's sword before the king, but the said earl refused, saying his ancestors had always been used to carry the city's sword. Lord Sheffield, hearing the dispute, said, " If he will not carry it, give it to me to carry," and the Lord Chamberlain replied, " Shall the king ride in state and have no sword carried before him?" The matter was therefore laid before the king, who decided that the Earl of Cumberland should carry the king's sword till he reached the city gate; but, once within the bar, should take up then the city's sword. Again, 1639, when Charles I. entered York in his progress towards Berwick, the city's sword was borne before him by the Earl of Arundel, Earl Marshal of England, because " Lord Clifford, who was chief captain of this city, was then absent, and in the King's service at the city of Carlisle, who of right should otherwise have borne the same. And afterwards, during the King's abode in the city, which was for the space of one month, the sword of the city was borne before the King by divers of the Lords in their courses severally, and not always by one and the same person, till the Lord Clifford came to the city, and then he bore the sword before the King, as of right due to his father, the Earl of Cumberland, who was then infirm and not able to attend the service."

The Cliffords, no doubt, exercised authority for several generations over the Tower and Castle, although their names are not specially mentioned. As the Castle was also the residence of the high sheriffs, they may at times have been its governors, and under them a constable would be appointed to have charge of the store-houses and magazines when the Castle held the king's goods and revenues for the north. None of these functionaries are mentioned in history or by name anywhere. Possibly the services they rendered, although valuable, were not brilliant, and they have sunk into obscurity.

The first authentic record of a gaoler or keeper of the Castle prison is that of the person who held the office at the time of the rebellion in 1569. His name was Oswald Wilkinson, and he was appointed in 1557, to be reappointed the following March jointly with one Robert Lee. Wilkinson is described as "the most pernicious, railing, and obstinate papist in all the country, and wore a golden cross." He went with letters to the Duke of Alva to ask him to give the rebels aid. The idea was to seize a port, and Hartlepool was selected. But Wilkinson was himself in 1570 tried as a traitor. He declared he was as "innocent as a child two years old;" but on the 28th of November, 1572, Oswald Wilkinson, late of York, and gaoler of York prison, was drawn from the Tower of London to "Tiborne, and there hanged and quartered."

Lee possibly kept his appointment for some time, but, about 1580-90, he was succeeded by Robert Readhead, gentleman, one of the "shewers in ordinarie of Her Majestie's chamber."

In an original and rare MS. of heraldry, kindly lent by Mr. W. Gray, Under-Sheriff of Yorkshire, 1879, William Dethick, Garter King of Arms, declares "he is to take generall notice and to make declaration and testimony for all matters of armes and pedegrees honour and Revalry, and having intellegence that Robert Readhead, gentleman, one of the shewers in ordinarie of Her Majesties Chamber now castellan or keeper of the Castle of Yorke, sonne of Bartholomew Redhed of Sheriff-hutton in the countie of Yorke seeking to advance his name and fortune—he William by order of our

Sovereigne Lady Queene Elizabeth, presents him with a coat of armes; dated the tenth day of May in ye ffortieth yeare of ye Reigne of our Soveriegne lady Elizabeth by ye grace of God Queene of England ffrance and Ireland, Defender of ye faith and anno Dom. 1598.

"WILLIAM DETHICK Garter
"Principall King of Armes."

The next on the roll of Castellans was Peter or Piero Pennant, appointed by charter of Elizabeth in the thirteenth year of her reign. The appointment runs, " Keeper of the goal and the office of keeper of the Castle of York, and the grass within the precincts of the Castle with all cellars, houses, barns, stables, gardens, and the property of all prisoners and persons by the mandate of the counsel with the fees purtaining to the office."

After Pennant's death the appointment was granted to Anthony Benin, the king's footman, in 1610. Whether or not he retained his office until the outbreak of the Civil War does not appear, but, at the time of the sieges of York, the Castle and Clifford's Tower was under the military command of Sir Francis Cob, who held it until the capture of the city by the Parliamentarians. After this, as the north was now quiet, York was all dismantled, and its garrison withdrawn, except that of the Castle, which was entrusted to the keeping of the Lord Mayor as governor.

Upon the restoration, Lord Frescheville was appointed governor, and held the place for twenty-two years; but at length, in 1682, made way for Sir John Reresby, who had long held the deputy's place.

Sir John Reresby took the oaths as Governor of the Castle and City of York on the 10th May, 1682. He was also Justice of the Peace for the Liberty of St. Peter. His Memoirs, which are well known, contain many references to the Castle and its associations.

"Oct. 23rd, 1681. That evening I met the King going to council, and desired him that a notorious robber, one Nevison, having broken the Gaol at York and escaped, he would be pleased to grant a reward of 20*l.* to those that would apprehend him, and to make it known by proclamation. The truth was, he had committed several notorious robberies, and it was with great endeavours and trouble that I had got him apprehended at the first; and since his escape he had threatened the death of several justices, wherever he met with them; though I never heard I was of the number. The King's answer was this: 'that a proclamation would cost him 100*l.*, but he would order 20*l.* to be paid by the Sheriff of that County to him that took him, wherever it was; and that it should be published in the Gazette'—which was the same thing. The rogue was taken not long after, and hanged at York.

" March 2nd. I told my Lord Halifax that the better to secure the Government of York, I was willing to purchase the present possession of the Government, if my Lord Frescheville would quit it for a reasonable rate, which it was not unlikely he would do considering his age and infirmity."

Lord Halifax for that reason advised him to wait, as did the king, who said Lord Frescheville could not live two months, being "burnt down to the socket or quite wasted."

1682, May 10th. He assumed the Governorship. "The envy of my being preferred to the Government of York showed itself by several little insinuations of those that apprehended themselves (fit) for it."

June 27th. He came from Thrybergh. "I went to Clifford Tower to take possession of it with the High Sheriff, Sir Michael Wharton, Sir Henry Marwood, and others, which I found in pretty good condition as to repairs and stores (powder only excepted and cannon).

"Oct. 17th. Received a letter from Colonel Legge, Master of the Ordnance, intimating that Sir Christopher Musgrave, Lieutenant of the Ordnance, was ordered to come down to York by the King to take a view of the condition of that garrison, which occasioned my speedy journey to that place. I got there early the next day, and, waiting upon the Lieutenant, he took the dimension and situation of the Tower and Castle; and told me that his Majesty would be at the charge to repair the defects of the Tower (especially the parapet, which was too weak), and to bring the river about it." By which it would seem as though there had been no wet moat till this date, or that it had silted up.

"February 10th, 1685. Accession of James II. The King was proclaimed by nine in the morning by my Lord Mayor, myself and the High Sheriff. The first did it in the usual places of the city for that ceremony; I did it to the garrison, drawn together in the Thursday market; and the High Sheriff did it in the Castle yard for the county.[2]

---

[2] It is not quite clear that it was only for the convenience of the High Sheriff that he used the yard of the fortress as

"April 2nd. I had a letter from my Lord President that he had spoken to the King, and found no reason to think there was any design to disgarrison York.[3]

"September 2nd. The garrison at York I formed at that time into this method." The distribution of the troops over the town is precise, but hardly concerning these papers; the reader is therefore referred to p. 365 of the Reresby Memoirs.

"March 7th, 1687. I removed with my family to York, the assizes having begun there upon the 5th. Four fellows received sentence

being the nearest spot he could come to outside the different liberties of the city, for the purpose of his proclamation, or whether, as the king's castles had been rejoined to the counties in 1377—1399, while they yet nominally remained Government property, anno 1685, he was not allowed to use the yard for such purposes as a standing protest or reminder that the Castle belonged to the county by the charter unrevoked of Richard, ch. 15.

[3] As the garrison, excepting in the Tower, of York was removed, and the forts were dismantled 1664, so they must have been renewed in the time of Lord Frescheville.

of death, and a poor old woman also had the hard fate to be condemned for a witch. Some, that were more apt to believe those things than I, thought the evidence strong against her; she was afterwards remanded. However, it is just to relate this odd story." [1]

So far the Memoirs as to any interesting points connected with the old Castle of York. On the coming of William and Mary, as Sir John held the place for James II., he was naturally turned out by force of circumstances, the Earl of Danby (November 26th) allowing him to go, under arrest, at large to his residence, Thrybergh Hall. Afterwards, through his firm patron from the first, Lord Halifax, he has an interview with King William, to whom he says, " Sir, if you have resolved to take away my two Governments of York and Burlington, I hope you will not expect I should wait on a single company" (keep command of a troop). He said, "No, he did not expect any attendance from me."

[1] See post, p. 226.

"March 28th. My Lord Halifax and my Lord Nottingham moved the King in Council that I might have the keeping of the Manor of York (residence of the Governors of York, near St. Mary's). But by the underhand dealings of my Lord Danby, who had certainly pressed him in it for Alderman Waller, late Lord Mayor of York, I received a flat denial, and with this reason of unkindness, that that Alderman had done something for the service of the present Government, Sir John Reresby had done nothing."

Six weeks later Sir John died somewhat suddenly, in the fifty sixth year of his age—12th May, 1693.

Between the date of Sir John's death and 1709, Messrs. John Butler and Ash acted as governors in succession; Mr. E. Chippendale to 1718; Mr. Thomas Ward from 1726 to 1731; Mr. Thomas Wharton, 1756 to 1772; Mr. William Clayton, 1781 to 1805. From 1689 to 1805, the appointment was recognized as in the sheriff's gift, on the ground that he was responsible for the safe custody of the prisoners, and should have the prison in charge of an officer of his appointment; so nominally the governors went out of office with the sheriff, and were open to reappointment in like manner as the under-sheriff. As time rolled on, the justices of the peace gradually contested the high sheriff's right to this patronage.[5]

Mr. Christopher Stavely succeeded to the appointment in 1805, and held it till his death in 1824, when Mr. Shepherd, one of a family which at one time furnished all the gaolers of Yorkshire, was appointed. He resigned in 1840, and it is said the magistrates nominated his nephew to succeed him; but the high sheriff, holding to his claim, appointed Mr. John Noble to the governorship, which he retained till his death in 1864. He was succeeded by Captain W. F. Lowrie, whose appointment was not op-

---

[5] In other counties the stewards of liberties by charter frequently enjoyed this privilege of nomination, and not the high sheriff.

posed by the high sheriff. On the 1st April, 1878, the prison of York Castle, with all others in the United Kingdom, passed to the direct control of the State; and upon the death of Captain Lowrie in June of that year, Captain A. W. Twyford, the present governor, was appointed by the Right Honourable the Home Secretary.

A distinction must, however, be drawn between the governor of the castle and the keeper of the gaol. Both offices, no doubt, existed from the earliest time, and probably the latter was the governor's deputy or castellan in time of peace. The gaoler's apartments were at the south end of the present Debtors' Prison, and continued to be occupied as such until the erection of the existing governor's house at the reconstruction of the prison in 1829. The governor's official residence was the building known as the Manor House, or the palace of the Stuart kings, the Castle itself being held by a deputy. This, which had been the residence

THE KING'S MANOR HOUSE.

of the last Abbot of St. Mary's Abbey, became, after the suppression of the monasteries, the head-quarters of the Lord-Lieutenant of the Northern District. The king and members of the royal family occasionally lodged at this house when on their way north or south. Charles I. lived here during his three months' residence in York; although he stayed in the city on three, if not four occasions. His first visit to the Manor House was in the spring of 1639, when on his way to the north. It was then under the charge of Sir Edward Osborne, the Lord President being still in Ireland. The following August the threatening attitude of the Scots brought the king again to the north, and the Manor House was again his abode. In November, 1641, Charles, accompanied by the Prince of Wales, spent two nights in York, residing with Sir Thomas Ingram, at his house in the Minster Yard. King Charles made his last visit to York in 1642, when he was again entertained by Sir Edward, as was Queen Henrietta Maria the following year, when she fled to York. In 1538, the Protestant Council of the North, permanently established by a Royal Commission, 1537, took up their abode in the King's Manor. Here also Henry VIII. resided with Catherine Howard, or rather in a temporary palace built by his order in the grounds of the old Abbey of St. Mary adjacent. Here, also, time of Elizabeth, resided Thomas Radcliffe, Earl of Sussex, as President of the Council of the North. And, in later years, it was in this house Lord Burleigh received King James and the Queen.

In 1609, Lord Sheffield expended 3000*l*. in alterations and additions to the buildings. In 1628, Wentworth, Lord Strafford, as President of the Council, occupied the house for many years, and here Lady Strafford died. During the siege of York, in 1644, by the Parliamentary forces, the house and grounds were wrecked. During the Protectorate the King's Manor was occupied by Colonel Lilburne, from which he went to less comfortable quarters at Newgate at the Restoration. After his time there was, as now, a general scramble for the rewards distributed by Charles II. In the time of James II., as the Reresby Memoir tells, Father Lawson nearly obtained possession of the buildings to form a college. But eventually, in the time of William of Orange, the room that had been the Star Chamber of the Council of the North, next consecrated for Roman Catholic worship, became the assembly-room for ladies and gentlemen coming to the assizes and races, and was also used as a common room of entertainment by the high sheriffs in those times. It still remains a Crown property, and is now used under a grant or lease for the beneficent purpose of a school for the blind, and bears the name of the Wilberforce School; poor little children now use the Star Chamber as a dormitory. On the walls of this chamber, over the old and original fireplace, may still be seen the royal badge of the Tudors, the crest of the

Hastings family, Earls of Huntingdon, the badge of the Earls of Warwick, afterwards taken by the Dudleys. The fireplace is said to be of the time of Elizabeth.

A portion of the old buildings undoubtedly belong to the old Abbey of St. Mary, such as the main staircase; other portions to the sixteenth century, built by the Earl of Huntingdon, Henry Hastings.

EXECUTIONS AND DEATHS.

CHAPTER IV.

EXECUTIONS AND DEATHS.

YORK Castle, as the principal prison of that great northern city, the centre and focus of all the movements in progress in the northern country, was in all ages crowded with prisoners. These belonged to many categories. There were political prisoners—those who, for conscience sake or the hope of aggrandisement, espoused the losing cause, and found themselves classed as traitors by the opposite side when it won. There were the victims of religious intolerance and superstition, stout-hearted professors of a faith which differed from that established by law, and for whom, whether Protestant or Papist, Jesuit, Nonconformist, or Quaker, very summary measures were generally the rule. There were others who, whether self-deluded or impostors fully conscious of their guile, traded upon the credulity of their more simple fellows and followed the dangerous calling of sorcerer and witch, notwithstanding the barbarous penalties detection entailed. There were large numbers of the impecunious and the unfortunate classes who, as destitute debtors, dragged out a miserable existence, having no hope of release but in death. Last of all, there were the criminals pure and simple, the law-breakers and depredators, who, whether committed for colossal offences or more commonplace crimes, expiated them alike upon the gallows tree. These were the days when the gibbet was in perpetual requisition, when traitors to reigning monarch or constituted authority, when recusants, so styled, who chose to worship God according to their own convictions, and not as others ordained, suffered the same fate with horse stealers, violators, money clippers, with reckless roysterers who drew weapons on

EXECUTIONS AND DEATHS. 91

one another at the smallest provocation, with the thieves who cut purses in a crowd, and with the robbers who infested the king's highway, and with those more truculent ruffians who, in pursuit of prey, or to slake their revenge, murdered fellow-creatures in various cold-blooded ways.

The assize records show that between A.D. 1370 and 1879 at least five hundred and sixty-four people were beheaded or hanged at York. From the earliest times executions took place upon the gallows of the Abbot of St. Mary's. In connexion with this abbey or monastery of St. Mary was that of Galmanho, and Hovenden says they were one and the same. Leland, speaking of the last, describes it as being built without the walls of York, at or near the place where in old times the city dirt had been deposited and criminals executed. Now the common instrument of execution in the Saxon times was the gallows, in Saxon *galga;* thence, as Lye shows, we get *Galman, Galmanho.*[1] But,

[1] Saxon Dictionary.

at the date above mentioned, it was resolved to deprive the monks of the doubtful privilege of carrying out the extreme penalty of the law. The alleged reason was a riot raised by the monks at the last execution. Therefore, on the presentment of the grand jury at the next assizes, and after a discussion by the bailiffs, magistrates, and others, a meeting was held at the Castle of York, on the 1st March, 1379, to consider the question. It was then decided to build a gallows on (or opposite to) Knavesmire, the present race-course, which, after its namesake in London, should be called the Tyburn of York. It was also resolved "that Master Joseph Penny, joiner, of Blake Street, in the city of York, do build the said gallows forthwith at a cost of 10*l*. 15*s*.," and these new gallows were completed by the 7th March. It may be mentioned here that the word "Tyburn," as known in London, is by some supposed to be a corruption from "Thief bourne," or "Thief's bourne." Another more fanciful derivation is from "Tie" and "Burn," in reference to the bonds and burning to which criminals were subjected. This, again, is refuted by Skinner, in his "Etymologicon Linguæ Anglicanæ." This writer asserts that the name is really derived from $Tυν$ and $Bυμηα$, which means the two burns, with reference to two neighbouring streamlets long since dried up. Holinshead states that, in Edward the First's time, the place was called The Elms, and that the name of Tyburn was adopted at a later date.

The new gallows were erected within a week of their being decreed, and, before the month of March was out, were used for the execution of Edward Hewison, a lad twenty years of age, who was a soldier of the Earl of Northumberland's Light Horse. Sentence of death was passed upon him for violating the person of a maid-servant belonging to Sheriff Hutton Castle. "Hewison, being the first man that suffered at the New Tyburn, caused a great number of people from the neighbouring towns and villages to assemble to witness his untimely end. After the execution, his body was hanged upon a gibbet in the field where he had committed the crime in Sheriff Hutton road."[2] To assist at public executions was a very popular amusement at York. There are numerous phrases to be met with in the official records, such as the following:—"Thousands witnessed the dreadful catastrophe;" "the ceremony was performed in the presence of thousands of spectators;" "it was computed that not less than six thousand spectators were present to witness the dying struggles." It was a day of general festivity; the scene of action, whether Knavesmire or elsewhere, was like a fair. It is recorded "that at the execution of two murderers at the gallows of St. Leonard's Dykes, outside Walmgate, the convicts and their guards could with difficulty pass down Castlegate, by reason of the great multitude of people with whom that street was crowded from

[2] "Criminal Chronology of York Castle," p. 2.

top to bottom, so that nothing could be seen but a forest of hats, and on the Pavement the people had to form a passage for the cart to pass through, the crowd pulling off their hats as the solemn cavalcade passed by. In turning to Fossgate the street was one mass of human beings. One woman had her leg broken in the crowd, and a young man had his thigh broken; both were taken to the doctor. On entering Walmgate, the same scene presented itself, but no accident occurred. The two culprits here fainted, and stopped before the house of Mr. James Addinale, the sign of the 'Golden Barrel,' when the good Sheriff ordered Dame Addinale to give them some mint water, and, after their recovery, each had a glass of wine, and then proceeded to the place of execution."[3]

Publicans whose taverns lay on the route, or near the scene of the crime, and where, as a general rule, the dead body of the criminal was

[3] "Criminal Chronology of York Castle," p. 27.

hung in chains, made their fortunes by selling ale to the crowd.

This brutal eagerness to witness the sufferings and degradation of fellow-creatures cannot but be strongly reprobated. But it must be remembered, as a blot upon our modern civilization, that, till within half a dozen years, crowds collected at the Old Bailey and elsewhere, as they had done from time immemorial, to see an unfortunate wretch turned off. Nevertheless, an ordinary execution by hanging, repellent as it must be to all persons of fine feelings, was very much less horrible than the methods formerly in vogue. To draw the condemned malefactor on a sledge or hurdle slowly along the streets was to prolong his agony and pander to the lowest instincts of the bystanders. But the actual infliction of the sentence was often still more horrible. The ruthless practice of burning for heresy was, as is well known, long practised in the fierce days of religious intolerance; but the same punishment was meted out to culprits guilty of petty treason—

a title given to the crime of husband murder. Wives convicted of this atrocity were liable to be thus punished, until the thirtieth year of the reign of George III., when the practice was abolished. The last recorded case in England was at Bury St. Edmund's, on the 25th June, 1788. As a general rule, the unfortunate woman was first strangled, but not always completely or successfully. Catherine Hayes, for instance, who was executed in 1726 for the most cold-blooded and atrocious murder of her husband, was subjected to the most horrible tortures before death supervened. It is recorded that "when the wretched woman had finished her devotions, in pursuance of her sentence, an iron chain was put round her body, with which she was fixed to a stake near the gallows. On these occasions when women were burnt for petty treason, it was customary to strangle them by means of a rope passed round the neck, and pulled by the executioner, so that they were dead before the flames reached the body. But this woman (Catherine Hayes) was literally burned alive; for the executioner, letting go the rope sooner than usual, in consequence of the flames reaching his hands, the fire burned fiercely round her, and the spectators beheld her pushing away the fagots, while she rent the air with her cries and lamentations. Other fagots were instantly thrown on her, but she survived amidst the flames for a considerable time, and her body was not perfectly reduced to ashes in less than three hours.[4] York was not without its cases of the kind, although nothing so horrible as the death of Catherine Hayes is mentioned. In 1650 Ann Crowther suffered in this way; hers was an almost incredible story. A three weeks' widow, she married another husband simply that he should reap her corn. Within forty-eight hours she turned him out of the house, having first given him a poisoned cake to eat, and barred the door against him, so that he died of poison, cold, and exposure combined. Ann

[4] "Remarkable Trials," p. 99.

Pinchbecke again, who in 1671 brained her husband while sleeping, with an axe which she had secreted under her bed. Mary Ellah, who strangled her husband in a fit of jealous excitement, was hanged at York Tyburn, and afterwards burnt near the gallows. On the 10th August, 1767, Ann Sowerby, of Whitby, was executed at York Tyburn for poisoning her husband. She was drawn to Tyburn from the Castle on a hurdle, there strangled and burnt. Ten years later, March 29th, Eliza Bordington suffers by hanging and burning for a similar offence; and these are the last occasions of strangling female criminals, and then burning their bodies in Yorkshire.

The execution of those convicted of high treason was carried out always ruthlessly, with many disgusting details. The sentence inflicted upon Andrew de Barclay, or Harcla, early in the fourteenth century, will serve to illustrate this. This unfortunate man had been created Earl of Carlisle for his services at the battle of Boro-

bridge in 1321, when he took prisoner the Earl of Lancaster, and many barons who were subsequently hanged, drawn, and quartered at York, John Lord Clifford, Roger Lord Mowbray, and Sir Joceline d'Ervil being among the number. But Harcla shortly afterwards conspired with the Scots and was unsuccessful. They executed him at Carlisle, after having tried him in his absence. He was allowed no opportunity of defending himself, but only brought up for judgment. The following was his sentence :—
" The award of the Court is that for your treason you be hanged, drawn, and beheaded ; that your heart and bowels and entrails, whence came your traitorous thoughts, be torn out and burnt to ashes, and that the ashes be scattered to the winds, that your body be cut into four quarters, one to be hanged upon the Tower of Newcastle, one on Carlisle, one upon the bridge at York, one at Shrewsbury, and that your head be set upon London Bridge for an example to others that they may never presume to be guilty

of such treason as yours against their liege lord."

Witness, again, the punishment meted out to the unfortunate leaders of the well-meant but entirely unsuccessful "Pilgrimage of Grace" in the reign of Henry VIII. Lord Hussey, one of the highest of these in rank, was first "hanged for twenty minutes, then cut down, stripped, and laid upon a stage built for that purpose close to the gallows, where his head was cut off, his body quartered." The same fate met the Abbots of Jervaulx, Ridaulx, and Fountains, also the Prior of Burlington. Robert Aske, Esq., escaped the mutilation of his remains, but after execution his body was taken to Master Robert Pyements, at the sign of the "Eagle and Child" in the Pavement, and there chains were fixed upon his lifeless remains. Next day the sheriff, escorted by a troop of light horse and a large number of citizens, took the body to Heworth Moor, where the corpse was suspended to a gibbet thirty-five feet high, there to remain for twenty years.

Simon Digby and other gentlemen were executed in 1570 on Knavesmire, and there "hanged, headed, and quartered. Their four heads were set on the four principal gates of the city, with four of their quarters. The other quarters were set up in divers parts of the city as a warning to rebels to avoid a similar fate."[5] The Earl of Northumberland, who rose against Elizabeth with the avowed intention of restoring the Catholic religion, and advancing Mary Queen of Scots to the English throne, was executed in the presence of a large crowd upon the Pavement at York. A scaffold had been erected at the east end of All Hallows Church, twenty-five feet long by fifteen broad, and twelve in height. His head was set on a very high pole. After addressing the people, he kneeled down and prayed for a short time, then rose and shook hands with those that were on the scaffold, but did not speak to them. After this he went to the fatal spot, knelt down with his

[5] "Criminal Chronology," p. 5.

face to the east, laid his head upon the block, and gave the signal to the executioner, who struck off his head at one blow. After his execution the head was set up on a very high pole, at the top of Micklegate Bar, and his body was buried in the Church of St. Crux in this city, by two of his servants and three women.[6] Hargrove adds, "The head of the Earl of Northumberland seems not, however, to have been taken down by official command; for in a curious old manuscript, written in those times, we find the following :—'In the year 1574 the head of the Earl of Northumberland was stolen from Micklegate Bar by persons unknown.'" .

After the suppression of this movement, the insurgents taken by Sir George Bowes, Lord Marshal of Elizabeth's forces, were executed wholesale. Stowe says he had it from Sir George himself, that he caused some of them to be executed in every market town and every public place from Newcastle to Wetherby. On

[6] "Criminal Chronology," p. 7.

Good Friday, March 27th, 1570, Simon Digby of Askew, John Fulthorpe of Iselbeck, Esquires, Robert Pennyman of Stoxley, Thomas Bishop, the younger, of Pocklington, gentlemen, were drawn from the Castle of York to the place of execution at Knavesmire, and there hanged, headed, and quartered. Their four heads were set up on the four principal gates of the city, with four of their quarters, and the other quarters were set up in divers parts of the county. As a general rule the custom was to take out the heart, still warm, and hold it aloft, saying, "Behold the heart of a traitor!" Sometimes to draw the entrails out, to slice the thighs, or quarter the bodies while the audience gaped and gloated over the performance, and sometimes gave vent to expressions of applause. Still more horrible and disgusting were the circumstances surrounding the execution of those sentenced for "recusancy," as it was termed, or wilful refusal to conform to the religion professed by the supreme authority for the time being.

EXECUTIONS AND DEATHS. 107

Bloody Mary's savage treatment of obstinate Protestants has been reiterated by historians till they have become household words. We· are less familiar with the atrocious punishments which Protestant Elizabeth and other staunch defenders of the faith tolerated and approved. To maintain in writing the Pope's supremacy was to be guilty of high treason, and to become liable under a statute of Elizabeth's reign—if a man, to be hung, but cut down alive, the breast and stomach sliced open, the heart still palpitating drawn out, after which, while yet warm, his limbs were to be hacked off, dipped in boiling pitch, and exposed over the gates on spikes. A woman for high treason was burnt alive. Margaret Clitheroe, for harbouring Jesuits and seminary priests, was committed to York Castle in 1586, was tried and sentenced to be pressed to death, which sentence was carried out with an unexampled barbarity. This is recounted at length by Mr. Baring Gould.[7]

[7] " Yorkshire Oddities," ii. 240.

The Puritan Parliament having, in 1642, forced Charles I. to sign the death warrant for the execution of two Popish priests, one of them aged eighty-seven, they were to be subjected to the usual indignities, but, after he had hanged them, the executioner refused to draw and quarter them, declaring he would rather hang himself. "At last a woman, full of more religious fanaticism than Christian mercy, urged and upbraided him so that he was wound up to a pitch of frenzy, and fell to work like a fury, cutting and slashing the bodies of both the martyrs, and hacking the entrails into small parts, flung them amongst the crowd."[8]

The fate of ordinary malefactors, who were merely hanged, was enviable in comparison. Many were supported to the last by the consciousness of celebrity, taking the large assemblage as a compliment to their eminence in crime, and often indulging in speeches of mock defiance and acts of bravado but little in keep-

[8] "Yorkshire Oddities," ii. 244.

ing with their awful situation. Thus Thomas Wilson, alias Mountain, who in 1570 killed the Abbot of St. Mary's, and stabbed the Archbishop of York, after all but escaping from Peter's Prison in the interval between sentence and execution, spent some time in addressing the crowd when brought under the gallows, was most reckless in his demeanour on the scaffold, and twice called out "God save the Queen!" before he was launched into eternity. William Borwick, who was executed for the wilful murder of his wife, coolly told the hangman that he hoped the rope was strong enough, as if it were to break with the stretch put upon it, and he should unfortunately fall to the ground, he might be so seriously injured as to become a cripple for life. Edward Wells, whose crime was forgery, took his hat, wig, and handkerchief off at the gallows, unbuttoned his shirt, then turned about, opened the noose of the rope, kissed it, put it under his chin, and would have thrown it over his head had not the fact of his being pinioned prevented him. The notorious Turpin (of whom more in a later chapter) appeared in a brand-new fustian frock and new pumps for his execution; he even hired, the day before his death, five poor men, at ten shillings each, to walk as mourners behind the cart which carried him to Tyburn. All the way he bowed to the numerous spectators repeatedly, and with the most astonishing indifference and intrepidity. "As he ascended the ladder, because one of his legs trembled, he stamped it down with an air of assumed courage, as though he were afraid of discovering any signs of fear. Having conversed with the executioner about half an hour, he threw himself off the ladder and expired in a few moments."[9]

There were even authenticated instances in which criminals adjudged to die, and actually executed, were restored to life because the ceremony was imperfectly performed. One of the most remarkable cases was that of John

[9] "Criminal Chronology of York Castle," p. 59.

Bartendale, a piper or strolling musician, who, on the 27th of March, 1634, was executed on the York gallows against Knavesmire for felony. When he had hung three-quarters of an hour, he was cut down and buried near the gallows. Shortly after, one of the Vavasours of Hesselwood, riding up, thought he saw the earth heave, upon which, with the help of his servant, "he dug the convict up all alive." Bartendale was reconveyed to York Castle, eventually obtained a free pardon, and turned ostler after his extraordinary deliverance.

Drunken Barnaby, in his "Book of Travels into the Northern Parts," thus hands him down to us:—

>Here a piper apprehended
>Was found guilty and suspended.
>Being led to fatal gallows,
>Boys did say, "Where is thy bellows?
>Ever must thou cease thy tuning;"
>Answered he, "For all your cunning
>You may fail in your prediction,"
>Which did happen without fiction.
>For, cut down and quick interrèd,
>Earth rejected what was buried;

> Half alive or dead he rises,
> Got a pardon next assizes,
> And in York continued blowing,
> Yet a sense of goodness showing.

When turned off, he said, flashes of fire seemed to dart into his eyes, from which moment he became insensible—till he woke up of course. Bacon records he knew " of an inquisitive person who hanged himself for the purpose of ascertaining if strangulation was a painful operation. One of his friends very fortunately cut him down before it was too late, when the curious experimentalist was quite satisfied that hanging was by no means painful or unpleasant, and that the moment strangulation took place, he had been struck with a flickering light, that was instantly followed by utter darkness." Various cases are recorded of individuals thus cut down, when hanged by accident or executed. In most instances they have asserted that they experienced a pleasant sensation on strangulation.

A similar case is that of "Half-hanged Smith," who was a Yorkshireman, although not executed at York. He was the son of a farmer at Malton, who had served both by sea and land. While a soldier in Lord Cutt's regiment of Guards, he became one of a gang of housebreakers, and was in December, 1705, arraigned upon seven indictments, for which he was duly sentenced to death. Great efforts were made to obtain him a reprieve, but all to no purpose, and on the 24th of the month he was hanged at Tyburn. Before he had hanged fifteen minutes the people called out " A reprieve !" and he was incontinently cut down, although no evidence is forthcoming of the actual arrival of the reprieve. When conveyed to a neighbouring house, bled and otherwise treated, he recovered his senses. His description of his sensations is thus given in the " Remarkable Trials," edited by Captain Benson, and published by Camden Hotten (p. 30) :—" When he was turned off he was for some time sensible of very great pain, occasioned by the weight of his body, and felt his spirits in a wild commotion, violently pressing upwards;

that, having forced their way to his head, he, as it were, saw a great blaze or glaring light, which seemed to go out at his eyes with a flash, and then he lost all sense of pain. That after he was cut down and began to come to himself, the blood and spirits, forcing themselves into their former channels, put him, by a sort of pricking or shooting, to such intolerable pain, that he could have wished those hanged that cut him down."

Such cases, says the same authority, were not uncommon at one time in Ireland, and persons were seen walking about whom it was well known had been only imperfectly hanged. It was then the rule that the body should hang for half an hour, but the sheriff, from "mistaken lenity, would look away after the prisoner had been turned off, while the friends of the culprit would hold up their companion by the waistband of his breeches, so that the rope should not press upon his throat." When the half-hour was expired, the deceased was put into a cart, which was driven at a gallop along a stony road. The jolting was considered a never-failing recipe for "bringing the patient to." One such recovery was so complete that the resuscitated man sat up in his coffin in the cart and gave three cheers. One of his friends was so much shocked by this indecent conduct, that he hit the ex-corpse on the head with his shillelagh and silenced him effectually. The blow killed the poor wretch, and the question arose whether the assailant ought not to be tried for murder; but, on taking legal advice, it was ruled that "no one could be successfully charged with the murder of a man who was already dead in law."

These are but a few among several cases that are well authenticated. In these times the theory that death should be caused by dislocation and not by strangulation has become the invariable rule. Death is therefore not only certain, but instantaneous. Were it not so, there might be some ground for the suggestion that, where burial follows so soon after execution, some medical tests should be applied, extending to the action of the voltaic pile on a bared muscle. Bodies buried have been found where the unfortunates had actually devoured the flesh of their arms in agony, hunger, and despair. Witness John Scott and the Emperor Zeno. The ancients held hasty inhumation in great dread. Plato tells of a warrior who was left for dead ten days on the field of battle, and who came to life when he was being carried to his grave. Asclepiades restored life to a man on the funeral pile, and Pliny relates the case of Lucius Aviola and Lucius Lamia, who showed signs of life upon the pile, under the action of fire, but they were too much injured to be saved.

Amongst the many ancient fancies regarding the dead was the belief of their being able to masticate in their coffin any substance buried with them. In old times, women were especially believed to be gifted with this post-mortem faculty of moving their jawbones very loudly, "claro sonitu." In this apprehension, that bodies buried alive might devour their own limbs, articles of food were interred with them. The fate of Abbé Prevost, author of "Manon Lescaut," is one in point. Passing through the forest of Chantilly, he was seized with an apoplectic fit; the body, stiff and cold, was found the following morning, and carried by some wood-cutters to the village doctor, who coolly there and then proceeded to open him; it was during this dreadful operation the wretched Abbé recovered, to expire soon after from the operation. Cullen mentions an hysterical woman who was deprived of movement and sensibility for six days. Licelus knew a nun of Brescia, who, after an hysterical attack, continued in an inanimate state ten days and nights.

In those early wild days no man could calculate on dying a natural death. Those who did not were scattered to the four winds, or were buried where they fell. The proportion of those said to have died in York Castle, supposed from natural causes, was small; 1638 gives 4; anno 1640, 15; anno 1641, 12; anno 1643, 57, among whom, one was Mr. Captain Ludley, buried in the chancel of St. Mary's Church, February 11.

One William Nevison, March 20th, 1638, and the names of several other Nevisons, proving that the family belongs to Yorkshire. But while there is no manner of doubt but that Richard Turpin, who has been credited with what was really the exploit of the notorious Nevison of Yorkshire, was an Essex rogue, it must be admitted that people of his name did live in York. Thus William Turpin and Dinah his wife, of Far-water-Lane, who died June 1st, 1812, aged 74.

1643, Grymstone, keeper of ye Castle, got rid of his wife under ye chancel of St. Mary's Church, July 7th.

One Peter Scarborough, hanged for "Clipping," and buried at St. Mary's, 25th February.

One John Nevison, buried March 16th, 1683.

Ten prisoners died in the Castle, 1708.

Six prisoners died in the Castle, 1710.

Seven during 1712.

1741, William Fountain, and Henry Sandyo, gentlemen, died and buried.

1746 was buried John Kay, who had been prisoner in the Castle 24 years; buried 20th May.

1750, buried from Castle, Rev. Francis Storey.

1751, Thomas Griffith, once Governor of the Castle, now a debtor, buried 10th November.

1756, buried Wilson Major, a prisoner, 100 years old, 25th June.

1761. Millicent Rasby, an old gentlewoman, who had been confined in the Castle 38 years for debt; buried her 2nd November.

1772. Joseph Brown, "Shearman" from York Castle; buried May 6th. Who or what a Shearman was it is difficult to decide.

1779. Thomas England, hanged for horse-stealing, and buried in St. Mary's churchyard, 13th August.

July 10th, 1783, died James Wilkinson, a prisoner for debt in the Castle for a space of 16 years, aged 73 years. The register states the distemper which caused death was "decay."

Likewise John Ellis, a debtor, died 27th July, aged 67; his distemper is put down as "wearing," probably worry. Between 1783 and 1803, many aged debtors obtained their release through "decay" and "wearing." Criminal prisoners died at about the rate of four a year; chief diseases—dropsy, fever, insanity, consumption, decay.

As doubtless there were many prisoners in a gaol so crowded as York Castle, who died at the various visitations of the plague, some reference to that terrible epidemic may not be out of place here. Quaint as are the recipes for the cure of the plague, more curious are the punishments prescribed for those who broke

EXECUTIONS AND DEATHS.

the rules laid down for stamping it out. Its introduction into England was generally laid down to the Scots, who, when in company with James I., are likewise credited with having presented England with a little insect more lively than a sober Scot. The Lord Chancellor of Scotland, Lord Dunfermlyne, in a letter to the Lord Chancellor of England, dated 30th October, 1606, writes of the plague:—"In Edenburght it hes bene continuall this four yearss;" its commencement, therefore, 1602. King James, with his followers, traversed England, reaching London 7th May, 1603, and on the 29th he issued a proclamation commanding all gentlemen to depart from the Court and city on account of the plague. (Cecil, State Papers, 1603—1610, p. 11.) King James, on his way, rested at Newcastle, which town was one of the towns inflicted thereafter. The plague raged in London from March to September, 1603. As the king did not enter till May, it was probably taken into the city by the baggage in advance. The disease appears to have been known in Scotland and the northern districts, however, fifty years before this time, as some alarm was occasioned a few years before the death of Queen Bess, by the appearance of the infection in the North Riding of Yorkshire. In July, 1603, Newcastle suffered terribly, and, notwithstanding the fattest and most responsible aldermen were made wardens of the gates to keep him out, Death stalked in and committed great ravages during December of that year with the inhabitants of York. But it was not till April, 1604, that this ancient city fully felt the disadvantage of dirt within its walls and all it disgorged into its rivers. Then indeed were issued vigorous orders. " No Bride beds were to be made." Not too many wives were to be allowed to resort to sick wives' labour ; not above twelve at most at one time. " A city officer was ordered to go through the streets and give warning to the inhabitants to kill their dogs, bitches, mastiffs, hounds, and

EXECUTIONS AND DEATHS. 123

greyhounds, and their cats, or else he would kill them." To encourage him in killing cats, he was to receive twopence and the skin. The pestilence was at its height in York during August—September, 1604, and when almost all who could fled the city, it is to the honour of its Lord Mayor, Thomas Herbert, that he remained, though he lost his wife, who was said to have been a good wife to him.

By the end of February, 1605, the disease died out, having, after all, only taken 3512 persons. The pestilence hung over the country at large until 1610; the deaths by it in London averaged 2000 a year. (Tracts relating to the Plague, 8vo, London, 1721, p. 60.) From these times till 1625 people recuperated. During that year 35,000 people died of the plague in London. As everybody, who could, fled from London as from York, so the infection was widely distributed during these four years, and in April, 1631, the people of the latter place got a scare by the appearance in the city of one Ralph

Best, who had escaped out of an infected house in St. Martin's Lane, London, and had reached York. It was determined that Best's goods should be burnt, and that he should be imprisoned in Monk Bar " till the change of the moon." Nothing more is heard of the wretched Best; perhaps they burnt him too.

About the middle of the month the Lord President of the Council of the North, Lord Wentworth, took up his residence at the royal palace, the Manor House, formerly a portion of the Abbey of St. Mary's—the house in which Lady Strafford died, and in which King Charles lived for three months while in York. Soon after Lord Wentworth's arrival, dreadful intelligence reached the city of a fresh outbreak of the plague in various parts of the northern districts. He well knew how to wake up an alderman, and by his order his secretary, Thomas Edmunds, addressed them; whereby, in consequence of which, according to their minutes, they took what appear to us very curious and

amusing steps. Minutes, 29th August, 1631—
" Whereas it hath pleased Almighty God to
visit some persons in St. Lawrence churchyard,
a few yards beyond Walmgate Bar (a number of
small, mean dwellings were clustered round it),
with the infection of the plague, so six watch-
men are set to watch the persons in the (so desig-
nated) churchyard, and to keep them therein."
" The constables are ordered to set all tinklers,
feather women, beggars, and all other wandering strangers, out of the city. No apple sellers,
nor other fruit or onion sellers to be admitted."
Stringent rules were ordered for nailing up the
houses of persons infected, at which they
rebelled somewhat, but the doors were nevertheless nailed up. "A constable going forth at
Micklegate Bar between ten and eleven o'clock
p.m., told a person it was not right he should be
abroad so late, to which ye Saxon, old Britain,
or Dane replied, ' He did not care a rush either
for him, the Lord Mayor, or aldermen,' and
volunteered to thrust his knife into him." For

this he was set in the stocks on the pavement, and set by the neck in the pillory, and whipped there.

A blacksmith's wife was whipped openly for saying, "if sickness would come in fast enough, she would run among the thickest of them." In the midst of death some persons were so reckless as openly to indulge in revelry and dissipation. One Coke, who, "in this dangerous and doleful time," was seen dancing and fiddling without Walmgate Bar, where the disease was rifest, was ordered to be openly whipped. Such cheerfulness was not to be tolerated, and people being frightened out of their wits, moulted at home, and died.

The city bellman was ordered to give public notice to the keepers of taverns and all houses not to receive any of the inhabitants to tipple or drink upon pain "that both drinkers and receivers should be shut up. Some lovers of the bottle induced the bellman to disobey his orders, and for this offence he was condemned to have his bell taken from him and to be committed to ward till he confessed who willed him to stay his cry for restraining all vinters and all house-keepers for receiving any to drink in their houses." That the disease of the plague is by ancient writers presented to us as breaking out in villages, as a rule, before cities, is a point worth noting even in 1879. Four women and one man, " who digged and raved up " clothes and other things that were buried in the ground, were set in the stocks, and taken out one by one, and set by the neck and hands in the Lyns and there whipped. The Lyns were irons fixed in a wall or post for punishing those who were rebellious and would not be ruled. Many were committed to the "little ease" for choosing to be cool and defiant at this time of trial.

When a person died, as supposed, of the disease, his body was to be viewed " by three or four honest women, whose verdict decided whether his body went to the pit or a graveyard with the Funeral Service." The oddest of all methods of treating the disease was to forbid medical men to attend those attacked. It was reported to the authorities that one, Richard Smith, a potter, residing in Micklegate, had died of the sickness. "An order was immediately made that no physician, apothicary, or other person professing the like art, should visit, or minister physic to any sick person without the Lord Mayor's licence."

Dr. Joseph Micklethwaite, his son and servants, had visited Smith; a peremptory order was issued that they should keep to their houses and not go abroad, "unless it were to take the aire on their backsydes," and they were to kill their dogs and cats.

Whatever may be thought nowadays of the Protectionist system, surely the remedies will seem more ridiculous. Probably the diseases of the plague and cholera are not far apart in deriving their origin from decomposed vegetable and animal matter in the air. It is not known to the writer whether the seasons during which the plague was at its worst were dry or wet; most likely they were very dry, following on heavy wet years. While learned and approved physicians were forbidden to approach those stricken, old dames were not. These, when acting as nurses, were advised to take all precautions, as appears from the following precepts which were issued. "1st. Let those poor people who are afraid to be infected by being employed about the sick, eat butter and bread, with sage, sorril, or garlic pilled, in the morning before their employment. 2nd. Let them put into their drink ginger sliced, and steep in it the tops of wormwood, first washed and burnt. 3rd. Let them shut in their mouths lettwall or angelico, or gentian," and so on, this last as a tonic being perhaps the most sensible order of the whole. There is no record, however, that these precautions were of much avail.

PRISON RECORDS.

K

CHAPTER V.

PRISON RECORDS.

YORK from the earliest times had many prisons. These were in proportion to its Liberties, each "Liberty" having a separate judicial establishment, with courts and officers of its own. Thus Monkbar was made use of as a prison for freemen of York. The Abbot of St. Mary's had his prison within the abbey precincts, for ill-disciplined or ill-conducted monks, and perhaps for freemen, inasmuch as the place of execution for criminals until 1379 was the "gallows of the Abbot of St. Mary's." The Tyburn, or "hanging up" of the bodies in chains, and the burning of them, being, as aforesaid, on the Clifton Ings low-lying meadows. It is likely, therefore, that such assizes as were held in those days were carried out in, or near to, this Abbey, until the Castle, being dismantled as a fortress, afforded the opportunity of erecting the courts as shown by Drake.

There was a prison, or dungeon, in or near to the chapel of St. Sepulchre, which stood on the site of the present Library of the Minster, anno 1818 (Hargrove). After this edifice had ceased to answer its purpose, in the reign of Queen Elizabeth, the chapel was sold to one Webster, and part of it was converted into a public-house, known as the " Hole in the Wall." On being pulled down, 1816, the workmen came to a dungeon some feet below the level of the ground.[1] This dungeon was approached by a flight of stone steps. Along the walls were the remains of iron staples, to which, in all probability, persons had been chained. Against the wall was a strong oaken frame, like modern stocks, which extended the whole

---

[1] The level of the Roman city is nine feet below the present one, 1879.

length of the dungeon This measured 35 ft. 8 in. by 9 ft. 4 in. broad, and was 9½ ft. high. As it was undoubtedly connected with the chapel, so it was the more likely used for ecclesiastical than for civil purposes.[2]

Then there was the prison and "Hall of Pleas" for the Liberty of St. Peter, where Quarter Sessions for the Liberty were regularly held. In those days the steward of the Liberty acted as the County Court Judge of the present day.

Coming to more recent times, there was the gaol for the sole use of the City and Ainsty, built 1807. In 1814, a "House of Correction" was built on a part of Toft's Green, or "Pageant Green," so called because the fraternity of Corpus Christi paraded there for their religious procession round the city, to perform the play of the crucifixion.

[2] Stocks can still be used as instruments to inflict pain. The last case in England was at the village of Rogate in Sussex, not fifteen years ago; and until very recently they were too freely called into play in the British West Indies (1879).

The state fortress of the Old Bayle became the Archbishops' prison. And last, there was the old gaol for debtors, perched on the old bridge—a shameful place, even in 1724, when it was taken down.

All of these prisons were doubtless open to the gravest reprobation. They shared with other prisons of the north of England the severe strictures passed upon them by Raine, who wrote the preface to the volumes published by the Surtees Society. He says,[3] "They were dens of iniquity and horror, in which men and women herded together indiscriminately. .... Some of them had no light and no ventilation; several were partly under water whenever there was a flood. .... Prisoners were at the mercy of the gaolers for their food and for everything they possessed. They had the meanest fare at the most exorbitant price. .... There was also the greatest inequality and injustice in the treatment of the prisoners.

[3] "Depositions from York Castle," xxxi.

Those that had money had many indulgences. They were allowed to go to places of amusement without the walls of the gaol, and some were even permitted to lodge beyond the precincts, subjected only to some trifling surveillance." Of all these dreadful dens the castle at Newcastle-upon-Tyne and the Prince-Bishop's prison at Durham were perhaps the worst. But the prison of York Castle was also in a most deplorable state.

"The number of prisoners who died in York Castle prison during this century is positively startling," says Raine. In these times all prisoners dying a "natural death"—not hanged, that is to say, or burnt—were buried in the churchyard of St. Mary, and, from a perusal of the parish registers, dating from 1604, it would appear that sixteen was the maximum in any one month, and, on an average of twenty-five years, there were about thirty per annum. The prisoners, although heavily ironed, were yet fighting always among themselves or attacking the warders. The deputy-governor—one Wilson—in the time of Nevison, and others like him, until the last forty years, maintained discipline and good order by swinging enormous keys, at the end of a chain, round and round, which caught a prisoner upon the head, at times, and knocked him senseless.

In July, 1658, the county of York was presented for not renovating the common prison. In 1677, this prison was almost in ruins. Previous to these dates the condition of wretched prisoners confined therein may be gathered from documents and state papers of the time.

Here is a petition from a worthy gentleman, Mr. John Wortham, whose lodging was not far from the prison walls. The petition is endorsed to the "Honourable Sir Robert Heath, kn., His Majesty's Judge of assize for the county of York, with my humble service, these present," and sets forth as follows :—

"My Lord—It had been fitter for me to have waited on you myselfe than to have presented my respects to you this way; but, my Lord, I have been so desperately ill these six weekes, I had hardly bene able to stir out of my bedde. My humble suit to your Lordship is in behalf of a great many poore distressed people that are now prisoners within the Castle of Yorke, that have noe thinge to subsist withall but the charity of well-disposed persons; and, as the case stands with them, the benefitt of what they have is very small, for they are not suffered to buy a bitte of bread, or dropp of drinke, nor so much as a halfepenny worth of milke, or a little fyreing in the wynter, but what they are compelled to buy of the keepers of the prison, where they pay twopence or threepence for that which is not sometymes worth a penny. My Lord, my lodginge being not farr from the Castle gate, the neighbours have made a great request to me to be a suitor to your Lordshippe, that at this assizes your Lordshippe would be pleased to make an order for these poore people, as formerly they have done, may send into the towne for such provision as they are able to compasse, where they may have it at the best hand. I hope your Lordshipp will pardon the bouldness of your most humble servant, John Wortham. From my lodginge this 9th day of August, 1642."⁴

Again the prisoners in 1654 made petition complaining of their gaolers, that " They have hindered divers prisoners from havinge their meate and drinke at the best hand, and to compell them to come to the high table, did lye some in dubble irons. That some prisoners sendinge for theire drinke within the castle, where they can have more for sixpence than they can have in the cellers for neenpence, the gaolers did abuse the prisoners, and tooke theire drinke from them and gave it to the lowe gaol prisoners. The gaolers' servant gets a share of the charities given to the prisoners. On July 10 last divers prisoners going to the Sessions at Malton, the gaolers refused to

⁴ In Preface to vol. 40, Surtees Society Publications.

divide the Cottrell bread, they were gone and others got their share. The gaolers doth refuse to hange up the stablistment of fees in a publique place, etc."[5]

No wonder that a great judge, Sir William Blackstone, should assert that the gaolers of those times were " frequently a merciless race of men, and by being conversant with scenes of misery steeled against any tender sensation;"[6] and this view is supported by one, who, in 1618, himself endured the discomforts of prison life, and published the same in a work entitled " Essayes and Characters of a Prison and Prisoners." The author, Geffray Mynshul, of Grays Inn, Gentleman, says (p. 60) "of jaylors:"

" Many men (borne well of gentle blood and extraordinary education) forsake the calm of their owne happy fortunes to arrive on those quick-sanded shores, and either by strength of purse or free gift of great persons, have such

---

[5] In Preface to vol. 40, Surtees Society Publications.
[6] " Commentaries," iv. c. 22.

place of command conferred upon them (I speak here of the better sort which are the Maisters) yet I know not whether the perverse unrulines of prisoners with whom they are to wrastle, or whether the fate of such star croste houses, or what other malevolent aspect sticks upon them; I know not I say whether one of these single or all of them together, alter soft and noble inclinations into cruel and crooked ones, neither is my complaint or condemnation of them generall, for I know some of this file may and doe march in the ranks of men, both worthy, and full of commiseration towards those poore people under their charge."

"But for the second sort, which properly jaylors are indeed, they are commonly base tradesmen that have broken, and by a little money pared off other men's goods buy such offices; els are they lazy serving-men, who, being weary of carrying the cloak-bagge, think it a brave life to come and command, as good and sometimes better men than their Maisters within the stinking precincts of a prison; and take the best choice you can, they are but outworne soldiers, but indeed for the most part the very off-scum of the rascall multitude, as cabbage carriers, decoyes, bum-bayliffes, disgraced pursoivants, botchers, chandlers, and a rabble of such stinkardly companions; with whom no man of any reasonable fashion but would scorne to converse."

In the same volume of the Surtees Society, a second petition is given, but without date, as follows :—

"For the worshipfull William Bethell, Esq., foreman of the grand jury for the county of Yorke. The humble petecion of the prisoners in the Castle of Yorke, complaining of the severall abuses committed and done by Thomas Core and William Crooke, jailors.

"Sheweth that contrary to the tables of severall fees and Acts of Parlement, the aforesaid jailors hath demaunded and taken severall sums of money for chamber rent, and likewise for our owne bedds and bedding, and doth compel us to pay for ease of irons (being in execution), altho' wee have paid the same to former jailors to whom wee was committed, lodgeing felons and debtors together in one roome or chamber, takeing more fees than one, viz., for every accion one fee, although wee are discharged from all such accions by the Sheriffe, takeing unjust fees from the prisoners when discharged, receiving 16*l*. and 8*s*. from six men committed and indicted for high treason at the last assizes, as fees due to them, besides 6*l*. for ease of irons, they or their servants takeing or receiving money at severall times from three persons indicted for murther, at Lent assizes last, promissing that the jury should acquit or discharge, and alloweing weekly out of the county bread a greater share to fellons and condemned persons than they doe to debtors. Alloweing condemned persons not only to dispose of it, but of most of the concerns in the jaiol. Tollerating persons condemned for high treason, for murther, for fellony, in execution, excommunication, besides 180 Quakers at the least, not only to go into the citty and county of Yorke, but to play-houses, taverns, coffee houses, &c. Not lodgeing in the jaiol above the number of ninety Quakers att any one time, from March last to July instant, takeing severall sums of money, besides bond and judgement, not only from men committed as misdemeanours, but from all sorts of felons, for ease of their irons.

"Wee distressed petecioners humbly crave to take the premisses into consideration, moveing the judges and justices of the peace, nott onely that the abuses may be regulated, but that a table of fees may be settled: and we shall be ever bound to pray, &c."

Debtors and others were allowed to lodge outside. Escapes were very frequent. Here is a statement dated March 9th, 1653, of Warders Thackeray and others; "concerninge the escape of six prisoners out of the prison of the Castle of Yorke. The saide prisoners were laide in the place called the low gaole, being supposed to be the safest place, and doubled ironed according to law. That the gaole being now known to be weake, the said prisoners did worke through the stone walle in one night, the weakness thereof was presented to the grand jury the last assizes. That the kayes belonging to the backe gates, soe called, of the saide gaole, were in the custody of the souldiery in Clifford's Tower, which obstructed the present pursuite of the saide prisoners, being in the night time."

While the workmen were engaged in works in connexion with the new building opposite the Court House they made a strange discovery. On the 8th July, 1780, while clearing away rubbish behind the Court House, they found a human skeleton laid about a yard distant from the wall, with the legbones enclosed with double irons. Eugene Aram, in 1759, when on his trial for the murder of Daniel Clark, in his ingenious defence, made a great point, as explaining Clark's disappearance, of the sudden and unaccountable disappearance of William Thompson, a felon who had escaped from York Castle. Hargrove says, " It is now fully believed that this was the skeleton of Thompson, and that in attempting to escape he had got to the top of the old Court House, by the assistance of a ladder which stood there, and in the descent had either been killed with the fall, or had so seriously injured himself as to linger out a protracted and most miserable existence. Either supposition is probable, for as nothing but nettles and high weeds grew on the ground where he fell, it was seldom or never resorted to by human beings."[7]

In a prison so shamefully kept, disturbances took place repeatedly and as a matter of course. Thus in 1761 there were 121 French prisoners confined in the Castle. On one night some of them cut away the bars of the windows, and

[7] " Hargrove," ii. 247.

twenty escaped over the walls. Six were recaptured, but fourteen were never more heard of. the 9th April, 1765, the felons rose on the under gaoler and turnkey, who were locking them up, taking their keys from them. They locked these officers into a cell, and attacked the outer lodge. On the porter refusing to give them the keys of the gates, they knocked him down. They also secured the governor, Mr. Wharton. The debtors came to the rescue, and recaptured the prison. During the fight the under-gaoler's leg was broken, and many were severely bruised. Hargrove relates that "the debtors, who prevented the escape of about twenty desperate villains, were rewarded by a general subscription in the city."

Smollet's account of York Castle is worth quoting, although his opinion on prison matters cannot be so valuable as was Howard's some four or five years later. Smollet writes in 1768, in "Humphrey Clinker," "The Castle (of York), which was heretofore a fortress, is now converted into a prison, and is the best in all respects I ever saw at home or abroad. It stands on a high situation, extremely well ventilated, and has a spacious area within the walls, for the health and convenience of all the prisoners, except those whom it is necessary to secure in close confinement. Even these last have all comforts that the nature of their situation can admit."

Until about 1835 debtors termed first and second class were allowed to roam with the deer over the Castle green all day. The female debtors prepared nice little dinners, and the two sexes were permitted to solace their confinement by dining and holding sweet communion together. Out of chaos order gradually grew, and towards 1865 all classes of debtors were confined to the male debtors' side.

Debtors of the third class, however, felt the full disadvantage of their situation. They were accommodated with felon fare, which consisted of the felon's cell, had rushes to sleep on, and were always exposed to the blast, for forty years ago windows or apertures for admission of light and air were not provided with horn or glass, and the wind and snow blew in as it listed. The reader is referred to the view of the Castle in 1737, where the iron railings run across and unite the two stone blocks. Facing the reader the two top landings on the right were occupied by aristocratic debtors; the dungeon in the basement on the left was the felons' prison, with the condemned cell in rear, in which horrid hole many people's ghosts ought now to walk.

The condition of prisoners confined in York Castle during the last century was probably no worse, but if anything better, than that of the inmates of other prisons in the county. But all that prisoners almost universally suffered before Howard's visitation and even long afterwards may be gathered from his own pages. It is a significant fact that in Howard's description of York Castle he states that the "Gaoler, Thomas Wharton (now William Clayton), re-

GATEWAY AT CLIFFORD'S TOWER.

ceived no salary." This does not mean that he served from pure love of the employment, but that his place was profitable solely on account of his fees and his licences to sell food and liquor to the prisoners. These fees are given as 8s. 8d. for debtors, and 9s. 6d. for felons, while all alike paid a fee of 3s. 4d. on admission to gaol. The gaoler also received ten guineas for every transport, but whether this was paid by the convict (and if so, it must have been like getting blood out of a stone), or by the State, or by the contractors to whom the transports were sold, practically as slaves to be deported to the plantations, does not appear.

Howard gives also the table of fees or rates which all prisoners were supposed to pay for their accommodation and food. This table was fixed from time to time, and seems to have varied little. It was duly approved by two of the king's judges or justices of assize, and countersigned by magistrates of the county. That quoted by Howard as in force at York

Castle is dated 14th July, 1735, being the ninth year of the reign of George II. It is signed by the Honourable Alexander Denton, Esq., one of his Majesty's justices of the Court of Common Pleas, and the Honourable William Lee, Esq., one of his Majesty's justices of the Court of King's Bench. It is countersigned by John Grimston, Ramsden Barnard, and Thomas Grimston, for the East Riding; by George Nelthorpe and N. Harvey for the West Riding; and by John Dodsworth, John Milbanke, and John Wastell for the North.

This list will be found *in extenso* in Howard's "State of Prisons," i. 399. It lays down the weekly charge imposed upon knights, esquires, gentlemen, yeomen, tradesmen, or artificers, for their commons. It was a sliding scale. The knight paid 13s. 4d.; the esquire, 10s. 4d.; the gentleman, 8s.; and the yeoman or tradesman, 6s. 8d. as his fee. The knight paid sixpence for his bed; so did the esquire; but the gentleman paid only fourpence, and from the yeoman twopence was deemed enough. It was furthermore ordered that "When the gaoler lodgeth two or more prisoners in one bed, they shall pay for their lodging amongst them after the rates above;" while "Every prisoner who provides his own bed and bedding shall have a room assigned suitable to his or their quality, and shall pay nothing for the same." Every prisoner was to be at liberty to "provide and send for victuals and drink and other necessaries from any place whatsoever, at all seasonable times, for their own proper use only, and not to sell the same." There was a commitment fee of two shillings required from every prisoner committed by the Judge in assize week. Other and much heavier fees were exacted from prisoners on discharge. The iniquitous custom of thus mulcting persons proved innocent was actually tolerated and approved. It was laid down that every person committed to gaol for suspicion of felony, or for misdemeanour, if found not guilty, should be discharged, "shall pay the gaoler for his discharging fee six and eightpence," with 2s. more to the turn-keys. If found guilty, and subsequently discharged by pardon, the discharging fee to the gaoler was 7s. 6d., and 2s. to the turn-key as before. If committed, but acquitted by proclamation, the fees were 2s. and 4s. Those who could not pay, whether innocent or afterwards pardoned, were detained *sine die* in gaol.

Over and above these, to a certain extent legitimate fees, there were other extortions practised, which were approved by no written law, but which were always ruthlessly imposed. "Garnish," as it was called, was the worst of these. Garnish, says Howard, is the cruel custom which obtains in most gaols of "prisoners demanding of a new comer GARNISH, FOOTING, or (as it is called in some London gaols) *chummage*. 'Pay or strip' are the fatal words. I say fatal, for they are so to some, who, having no money, are obliged to give up part of their scanty apparel; and if they have no bedding or straw to sleep on, contract diseases which I have known to prove mortal." To this garnish, when paid up by the new comer, other subscriptions were added by the old hands, and the whole sum was forthwith spent in liquor for a drunken debauch, which lasted the whole of the following night. The rate of garnish varied. At Whitechapel Gaol, in 1775, it was ruled that " Every person who comes into this prison as a prisoner shall pay for his garnish 2s. $10\frac{1}{2}d$." At Derby it was 3s. 6d.; at Richmond (Yorkshire), 2s. 4d.; while at Chelmsford, where no sum was specified, the notice was "that prisoners must pay garnish or run the gauntlet."

So grievous was the condition of prisoners in these times, that they became to some extent the care of the charitable, who bequeathed sums, not excessively large it must be confessed, to be expended upon these unfortunate people. Howard gives a list of the prison charities which had been given to prisoners in York Castle. Lady Lumley left seven pounds yearly, to be given on St. Thomas's Day, and paid by the Lord Mayor of York. "The honourable and ancient city of York" gave half-a-crown weekly in bread. Mrs. Francis Thornhill for straw—the only bedding prisoners were generally allowed, and not always that[8]— the annual sum was thirty shillings; and "the Lord Mayor of York had thirty pounds in his hands for this purpose." Dr. Phineas Hodgson paid two shillings weekly in rolls "to all that hear sermons." This has been modified in modern times, and inasmuch as the regulated allowance is deemed sufficient, the money for the sermon is paid to the chaplain who preaches. Two other bequests—Alderman White and Mr. Bowes—provided a quarterly sum for bread.

[8] Hargrove however says, "Every cell in this prison is provided by the county with an iron bedstead, a flock bed, and rugs; on each of which beds two felons generally sleep." ii. 237.

And besides these there are donations recorded by which destitute debtors were discharged. Mrs. Mary Lawson, of Micklegate, left 100*l.* by will to discharge a certain number of poor prisoners, whose debts did not exceed 20*l.* each, and with this grant thirty-two prisoners were released. Likewise, "the Right Honourable Richard, Earl of Burlington, and Sir George Saville, Bart., gave each of them ten guineas for the like use—with which twenty guineas the Rev. Mr. Kayley, ordinary of the said gaol, discharged eighteen prisoners."

POLITICAL PRISONERS.

CHAPTER VI.

POLITICAL PRISONERS.

IN the old troublous times, when conflicting factions struggled perpetually for supreme power, the adherents of either side suffered according to its fortunes, and were now at the top of the wave, now submerged and condemned to imprisonment or death. At York, as has been shown, the scaffold and gallows were always busy, and its prisons constantly full. In the records of the latter, and in the names of those executed, we read the passing history of the time. From the Welsh insurgent Rees ap Meredith, who was hanged at York in 1291, to the Jacobites who were " out " with Charlie Stuart in the '45, it is much the same story. The ringleaders of unsuccessful rebellion, taken red-handed and with their followers, were condemned, after a short shrift, to die as traitors. The story of the first of these is told quaintly in the pages of Holinshed:—" In this year, 1286, fell variance between the lord Paine Tiptost, wardeine of certaine castels in Wales, and a Welsh knight called Sir Rees ap Meridoc, so that sundrie skirmishes were foughten betwixt them and men slaine on both sides, to the great disturbance of the countrie."

The disturbance had been occasioned by a summons sent by the king's steward in Wales to Rees ap Meredith to appear " at the counties and hundreds." Edward wrote and desired Rees to keep the peace, but Rees, "having already put armour upon his backe, would not now incline to any peace; but to revenge his cause, assembled a great multitude of Welshmen, with whose help he burnt and destroyed many towns in Wales." The king therefore ordered the Earl of Cornwall, his lieutenant in England during his absence in Aragon, to "resist the malice and riotous attempts of the Welshmen." An army accordingly marched into Wales, and, "chasing the said Rees, dispersed his armie and overthrew or razed his castles." Rees himself went free, however, and continued in the same courses two years more. Whereupon Robert Tiptost, " using both speedie diligence and timelie counsell, gathered all such power as he could make, and passed forth against his adversarie." Rees met him in the open field, and, relying upon his superior strength, attacked the English. The Welsh were, however, beaten back, and, being attacked in their turn, were presently sorely discomfited. " Meridoc himself was taken, but the most part of all his army was slaine, to the number of four thousand men. Thus were the Welshmen worthily chastised for their rebellion. Rees ap Meridoc was had to York, where at length, after the king was returned out of Gascoigne, he was hanged, drawen, and quartered." [1]

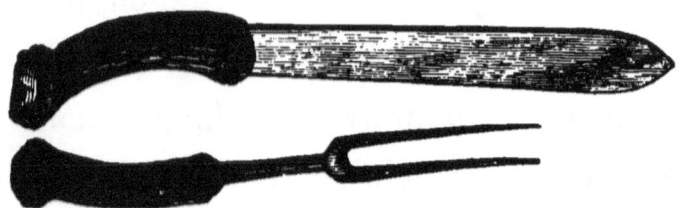

Photograph of the first and last knife and fork used in York Castle prison for drawing the entrails, and quartering the bodies of persons so condemned to suffer.

It was the same alternately with the chiefs of the Houses of York and Lancaster. While the Red Rose was in the ascendant, the Duke of York is beheaded, and " his head, which had boldly aspired to a Golden Diadem, was crowned with paper in Derision, put on a long Pole, and placed on the top of Micklegate Bar, with his face to the city," [2] so that, as Queen Margaret says in Henry VI., " York may overlook the Town of York." Next year the younger Edward, afterwards Edward IV., coming victorious to York from Towton field, removes his father's

---

[1] "Holinshed," ii. 489, 599.
[2] "History of York," i. 194.

head and substitutes those of several noblemen, the Earl of Devon, the Earl of Ryme, and others. Next, when Yorkshiremen rose against the land tax levied by Henry VII., and were in due course overpowered, the moving spirit of the insurrection, one John a Chambre, " a fellow of mean degree, who bore much sway amongst the common people, and was a perfect *Boutefeu*,"[3] was executed in great state in York. The chronicler records how he was hanged on " a gibbet raised a stage higher than ordinary, in the midst of a square gallows, as a traitor paramount; and a number of his men that were his chief accomplices were hanged upon the lower story round about him."[4] How it fared with the Yorkshire leaders of the Pilgrimage of Grace—Robert Aske, Lord Darcy, Lord Hussey, Sir Robert Constable, and several dignitaries of the Church—has been set forth in the previous chapter. The hand of Henry VIII.

[3] " History of York," i. 233.
[4] " Stowe's Chronicle."

was heavy upon them. Their offence was treason, no doubt, but they were animated by real patriotism and the love for old institutions. No blood was shed in the rising; the great host which had assembled to back up their opinions by the force of numbers dispersed rapidly upon the king's promise that he would listen to their requests. But Henry's temper could not be satisfied with less than the exemplary chastisement of the leaders of the movement, and this in spite of the pardons he had vouchsafed. All were sentenced to death, and, of the whole number, three, Robert Aske, Lord Hussey, and William Wode, Prior of Bridlington, suffered at York. The Castle was their last resting-place, whence, as usual, upon the sledge or hurdle, they were dragged to the place of execution, and there, with much fortitude, met their fate. Aske, from his scaffold on the Pavement, " asked the people to pray for him, and remember their rights and privileges, as true-born Englishmen, and not to be deterred by his death, for he had done no more than was his duty."[5] Lord Hussey spoke out no less bravely, saying he "hoped the period was not far distant when every Englishman would have the rights and privileges which they now required and were contending for, as he had only done his duty, and was about to seal his testimony with his blood."[6]

The fate which overtook the Earl of Northumberland and his followers in his rebellion against Elizabeth in 1569 has already been described. Northumberland was executed in 1572. Next year ten more Yorkshiremen—two of good degree—were also executed for high treason; but what was the nature of their offence, the records do not show. After which, until the conclusion of the struggle between Charles and his parliament, York saw the end of no political offenders. But York Castle was continuously full of political prisoners.

[5] "Criminal Chronology of York Castle," p. 3.
[6] Ibid., p. 3.

York during the early years of the Civil War was loyal to Charles, and all, therefore, who were of the opposite way of thinking fell into trouble. Words and phrases of seditious import were promptly taken notice of. Thus one Thomas Stafford was committed in January, 1640, for saying that the "Souldgeares were all roges .... that the Kinge and Queene was at masse together .... that hee is fitter to be hanged than to be a kinge, that he hoped ere long Lashlye (the Scotchman, Sir David Lesley) would be kinge, for he was a better man than any was in England."[7] Again, Thomas Waikefield deposes on June 9th, 1642, that he "hard John Troutbeck say the King was halfe French, half Germaine, and that he could live as well without a king as with a king." But in the surrender of York to the Parliamentary forces in July, 1644, the case was entirely changed. It is now the king's

[7] "Depositions from York Castle," Surtees Society, vol. 20.

partisans who are deemed offenders. The case of Colonel Morris, ex-governor of Pontefract Castle, was one of the most conspicuous. Morris was a Yorkshireman of position and a good soldier, who having at first served the Parliament, changed sides, and distinguished himself greatly by his surprise and seizure of Pontefract Castle for the king. He accomplished this by entering the Castle with nine associates, disguised as ordinary villagers, who brought new bedding for the garrison. No sooner were they past the gates than they fell upon the guards, "tumbled them into a dungeon, surprised the governor in his bed, and the Castle was won."* Then Royalists from all the country side flocked to the Castle, which was strengthened and revictualled under the orders of Colonel Morris, who was appointed governor. Cromwell, however, hastened "into Yorkshire, to Pontefract or Pomfret, a strong place which had been surprised in the begin-

* "Surtees," vol. 40. p. 14, note.

ning of the year, and is stubbornly defended."[9] It held out till March, 1649, when it surrendered, six persons being especially excepted from the conditions. Among them were the governor, Colonel Morris, and two officers suspected of having a hand in the death of Colonel Rainsborough at Doncaster. These six were, however, told they might cut their way out if they could. One was killed in the attempt; Colonel Morris and Cornet Blackburn made good their escape; and the other three, driven back into the garrison, were walled up alive by their friends, fed for a month, and eventually smuggled out of the Castle.

Morris and Blackburn got away into Lancashire, but were captured a few days later, and carried to York to be tried, although General Lambert had promised them their lives if they could escape from the Castle. They were brought before the Assizes in August, 1649. Thorpe and Puleston were the judges. The

[9] Carlyle's "Cromwell," ii. 71.

whole of the proceedings are given at length in the State Trials. Colonel Morris produced his appointment as governor of Pontefract Castle, signed by Prince Charles, as captain-general under his father. But he was treated as a common malefactor, and ironed before the verdict was found. There was no hope of acquittal for the prisoners, and both were sentenced to die. Yet the night before their execution both nearly made their escape from York Castle. Morris let himself down from the Castle wall; but Blackburn, following the same way, broke his leg. Morris, like a gallant gentleman, would not desert his friend, and both were easily recaptured.[1] Next day they suffered at the Tyburn without Micklegate Bar.

This was not the first visit Judge Thorpe made to York. He had been sent down in the previous spring to deliver the gaol, and in his charge to the grand jury had been at great pains to justify the recent condemnation and

[1] Raine, note, p. 15, Surtees Society, vol. 40.

execution of the king, and to vindicate the Parliament in all their proceedings. "In order to make the change from the king's name in forms of law, which it had ever run in, to the Commons of England, acceptable to the people, he raked up all the invidious and scandalous invectives against kings and monarchy, which the most celebrated Republicans to his time had ever wrote." The result of this Assize was the execution of fourteen men and seven women; the whole of the former having been convicted of treason and rebellion; the latter, of various crimes. Among these women was Emma Robinson, known in the neighbourhood as "Fair Emma," from her good looks, who, from jealousy, had poisoned a fellow-servant; another, Jane Lickiss, had strangled her servant-maid while in bed. Two were convicted of arson; Grace Bland had set fire to a public, known by the sign of the "Maypole," which was burnt to the ground, and Ellen Nicholson set fire to her master's house, which, with furniture, outbuildings, horses, cattle, and stacks of wheat, hay, barley, and straw, was completely consumed. But the strangest and most repulsive case at this assize, was that of Isabella Billington, aged thirty-two, who was sentenced to death for crucifying her mother, at Pocklington, on the 5th January, 1649, and offering a calf and a cock as a burnt sacrifice, and her husband was hanged (but probably on another occasion, as his name is not recorded) for being a participator in the crime. The whole of these sentences were carried out simultaneously. The culprits were taken in procession to Knavesmire; the men on sledges, seven on each, guarded by the sheriff's officers and twenty-four dragoons; the women in two carts, guarded by fifteen dragoons on each side. "On entering Castlegate that street appeared one mass of human beings, and the solemn procession was stopped for some time before it could proceed, the people were so closely jammed together. The whole of the twenty-one culprits joined as one voice in singing psalms from this street to the gallows." "It was a most awful scene—a terrible day, and thousands witnessed the catastrophe."[2]

Close watch was now set upon malignants and the expressions they used. It was not the custom to punish seditious language very heavily, committal and a short incarceration being followed by fines or orders to enter into recognizances to keep the peace. But the commonwealth did not choose that signs of disaffection, even to the extent of empty threats and idle words, should be passed over unnoticed. After all, the offences as recorded did not amount to much. One is arraigned for saying "that Generall Cromwell had lost his army . . . . and that he hoped within a twelvemonth to see Generall Cromwell's head off, and all the heads of all Parliament men in England that now is."[3]

[2] "Criminal Chronology," p. 29.
[3] Surtees Society, vol. 40, p. 39.

Another is charged with "drincking a health to Prince Charles, King of Scotts, and to his good success in England, and to the confusion of all his enimies."[4] "There are fortie thousande cavaliers coming into England . . . ." says a third, who is outdone by that staunch royalist Andrew Hudleston of Hutton John, Esq., who wishes "he had the keye of the Parliament House in his keeping, and he would keep both the Lord Protector and the Parliament till hee had cut their throats or they his." The Lord Protector again is stigmatized by Richard Browne as "a murtherer, and if he and his states had their due deserts, they deserved all to be either hanged or headed, for they had both headed the kinge and hanged many gallant and better men than themselves, only for getting their estates, that they might live in pride as they now did, and kept a company of rogues and excisemen and such like, to abuse the country still."[5] A stranger deposition is that which

[4] Surtees Society, vol. 40, p. 50.   [5] Ibid., p. 73.

hints at the presence of Prince Charles in Yorkshire disguised, in 1657. One Matthew Vasey meets a Mr. Anderson riding a fine horse, and asks him to give it King Charles, promising that it should be "five hundred pounds in his way another day. And the said Vasey did tell this informant (Mr. Anderson) there were three men who came from Bridlington-ward the other day, over about that place where his, the said Vasey, his dwelling is, and one of these men was thought to bee King Charles, ... the said men did lye down on a bedd there, and got some potchett eggs, and went before day northward upon horses, each of about ten pound price."[6]

But now there are symptoms of a turn in the luck. The last malignant called to account at York appears to have been Mr. William Elslay, who was informed against for saying he had a "commission from Charles Stuart to be captaine of a troope of horse in Sir George Booth's busi-

[6] Surtees Society, p. 79.

ness," and profferred—to the informer—a corporal's place. Sir George Booth, of Cheshire, headed the first movement in the north of England against the Parliament, but was unsuccessful. The Restoration was, however, near at hand, and with the accession of Charles II. the character of offences changes. Now it is an old woman against whom a true bill is found on the 13th May, 1660, for crying, "What! can they finde noe other man to bring in than a Scotsman? .... I hope he will never come into England, for that hee will set on fire the three kingdoms, as his father before him has done. ..... I hope to see his bones hanged at a horse's tayle, and the doggs run through his puddins." Charles II. was not popular from the first with a large section of his subjects. Parsons preached against his accession, declaring that he would bring back Popery and superstition; others openly swore that "Cromwell ruled better than the king ever will;" and others were outraged by the vice and dissoluteness which soon grew rampant in the new Court.

Very early in the reign there was a determined attempt at rebellion against the new *régime*. This occurred in October, 1663. The conspiracy was widespread, and comprised great numbers of the powerful Presbyterian party throughout the north. It was organized at Harrogate and Knaresborough, but its ramifications were spread through the whole of the northern counties. There were to be simultaneous risings— one in Westmoreland, under Captain Atkinson, an old Parliamentary officer; another at Durham. The object of the insurgents was to seize the garrisons of the north, and arrest the chief members of the Royal party. "They would then have endeavoured to effect an alteration in the government, setting up liberty of conscience, overthrowing the taxes, pulling down the bishops, and stopping the payment of tithes and other obnoxious imposts."[7] The Yorkshire

[7] Surtees Society, vol. 40.

insurgents appear to have printed a declaration calling upon the people to rise up, and join the noble band of staunch patriots, and defend their rights against injustice and oppression. The declaration began, "If there be any city, town, or county in the three nations that will begin this glorious strife;" and it went on to set forth that the object of the insurgents was to redeem themselves from the Excise and all the subsidies, to establish a Gospel magistracy and ministry, to restore the Long Parliament, and to reform all orders and degrees of men, especially the lawyers and clergy.[8]

Only the Yorkshire rising came to a head. There were no leaders of note or acknowledged ability, although great names, such as Fairfax, Wharton, and Manchester, were freely used, as though they were a party to the plot. The Durham movement was nipped in the bud; that in Westmoreland began and ended in a single night. But the Yorkshire men took up

[8] "Criminal Chronology," p. 33.

arms, and assembled at Farnely Wood, near Leeds. The insurgents actually threw up entrenchments, but did not hold out after daylight. Being few in number, and those ill-provided with arms and badly advised and officered, they passed away to their homes without any shedding of blood. They could make no head against bodies of regular troops and of the county militia, led by the cavaliers, prompt to hold by force all that they had so recently regained.

Great numbers of the insurgents were speedily arrested and thrown into prison. A special commission, consisting of Sir Christopher Turner, Baron of the Exchequer, Sir John Keeling and Sir John Archer, Justices of the Common Pleas, was sent down to York in the depth of winter to try offenders, of whom twenty-two were executed at York, and four at Appleby. Raine, in his preface to the fortieth volume of the Surtees Society, gives the names of those who were hanged, and drawn, and quartered. Among them were Captain Oates, of Morley; John

Ellis, of Morley; and Robert Oldroyd, of Dewsbury. They were most of them West Riding men, engaged in the manufacturing industries for which that part of England was even then renowned. Richard Oldroyd, known as the devil of Dewsbury, was executed the following year. Captain Atkinson, Waller, and others, who were executed at Appleby, were the leaders of the abortive Westmoreland rising. A number of other insurgents were acquitted, but bound over to find sureties for their good behaviour, and to take the oath of allegiance. Twenty-nine were ordered to be kept in gaol without bail, till the delivery of the gaol, for high treason. Among them were William Stockdale, of Bilton Park, Esquire; Henry Pownall, of Hawnby, gentleman; Thomas Lascelles, of Mountgrace, gentleman; James Fisher, of Sheffield, gentleman; and John Joblin, of Newhouse, gentleman. Twenty-seven more were freed by proclamation, but had to find securities, and to take the oath of allegiance; while fourteen were ordered to find bail to appear at the next assizes, and were in the meantime to be of good behaviour. Lastly, ten unfortunates were sentenced to remain in York Castle without bail, where many of them lingered on for several years. On July 25th, 1664, Ralph Rymer and John Hodgson were ordered to be imprisoned for life, and all their goods and lands forfeited; but Hodgson was released and pardoned the following March. John Joblin, who had given promises of help to the Durham men, was actually the gaoler of Durham Prison. He was imprisoned at York for several years.[9]

None of the above-mentioned, whose names Mr. Raine gives with so much particularity, tally with those recorded in Mr. Knipe's "Criminal Chronology of York Castle," as having been executed at York on the 25th January, 1663 (? 1664) for complicity in this same plot. These, eighteen in number, mostly men of Leeds, Otley, Poppleton, and Rufforth,

[9] Raine, Surtees Society, vol. 40, passim.

are described as conventical preachers and old parliamentarian soldiers, and they were undoubtedly engaged in the Farnely Wood plot. Two of them, but their names are not particularized, were quartered, and their heads and quarters were set up on the several gates of the city. Four of their heads were placed over Micklegate Bar, three at Bootham Bar, one at Walmgate Bar, one at Monk Bar, and three over the Castle gates. Three others were also tried and executed at Leeds.

Both before and after this insurrection the informers were busy at their despicable trade, and the depositions show that all who dared to speak in favour of the past, or against the present *régime*, were certain to be denounced and brought to justice. One was committed for saying, " It was a good day when the king's head was cut off. There hath been no peace like as was in Oliver, the Protector's, time. It is a pity butt that all kings' heads should be cut off." There were many who remembered Cromwell with loyalty and affection, and drew comparisons unfavourable to Charles II. Even Pepys, in 1667, writes, "It is strange how everybody do nowadays reflect upon Oliver and commend him, what brave things he did, and made all the neighbour princes fear him; while here a prince come in with all the love, and prayers, and good liking of his people, who have given greater signs of loyalty and willingness to serve him with their estates, than ever was done by any people, has lost all so soon." "There was never a king in England that was a chimney-sweeper but this!" cries a yeoman's wife. Walter Crompton is denounced for clapping his hand upon his horse's buttocks, and saying, "Stand up, Charles III., by the grace of God; which is an usuall expression of the said Walter Crompton's." "People groaned under Charles' taxation." "There will be money spilt before the assessments be paid." "Hee sent first to see what we would give him, then he sent for money for our heads, and lastly for sesements, soe he intends to send soe long till he makes us all beggars like to himself." What made the bearers of the burden chafe the more, was the profligacy and debauchery in which these heavy imposts were wasted when raised. These complaints against the king and the new monarchy increased as the reign wore on; but, as the records show, the charges for seditious words became fewer. Later the arraignments were chiefly for recusancy, against Nonconformists and Quakers, the seminary priests and those who harboured them, while some few people of note were tried on charges of high treason, for seeking to re-establish the Roman Catholic religion; with these the next chapter deals more in detail. The trial of Sir Thomas Gascoigne at York, in 1679, is one of the most prominent of these. He was then eighty-five years of age, and the chief evidence was that of one Bolron, a notorious informer in the northern counties, who had been in the baronet's employ, but had been dismissed for peculation. The witness declared that he several times heard consultations for "killinge the kinge and promoting the Roman Catholic religion, and establishing a nunnery at Dolbauke, near Ripley." The chief personages at these consultations were Sir Thomas Gascoigne, his son Thomas, John Middleton, of Stockhill Hall, and others. Bolron's statement was supported by Lawrence Mabury, or Mowbray, who had been a footman in Sir Thomas Gascoigne's service. However, in spite of their vile machinations, Sir Thomas was acquitted, and so was his son. It was at this period, in the latter part of Charles II.'s reign, when the statute of præmunire was put in force, that the Castle of York, the Ouse Bridge, and other prisons, were crowded with Roman Catholic prisoners, all of whom were released, however, during the brief ascendancy of their opinions under James II.

Except in the two Jacobite movements of 1715 and 1745, England had peace from political dissensions after the Revolution of 1688. With the first of these York does not appear to have had any connexion, but the second was long remembered there. The nobility and gentry, headed by the Archbishop of York, Dr. Herring, entered in an association to raise money, and aid in the defence of "his Majesty's Government and person in general, and of the county in particular." Upwards of 30,000*l*. was subscribed, and the city of York raised four companies of men, styled the Yorkshire Blues. The various wards, for the further security of the city, organized themselves in bodies properly clothed and accoutred, which remained under arms for ten months. The Duke of Cumberland, after Culloden had ended the Pretender's hopes, halted a day at York on his way southward, and was received with the usual honours, banquets, deputations, addresses, and the freedom of the city. He left behind him a large batch of prisoners, all of whom were tried at York, and many executed in the autumn of 1746. They were mostly Scots. One Irishman, Crosby, of Colonel Townley's regiment, was reprieved. Part were taken from the Castle on sledges on the 1st November, 1746, to the Tyburn. "As they were coming down Castlegate, Mr. Duct, one of his Majesty's messengers, brought a reprieve for John James Fellens, who was immediately taken out of the sledge, and conveyed back to the Castle." The culprits were first hanged, then, after an interval of ten minutes, taken down, laid upon a table, and stripped naked. "Captain Hamilton was the first whose heart was taken out, which the executioner threw into the fire, crying out, 'Gentlemen, behold the heart of a traitor.' When he came to the last man, which was Frazier, he said, 'Gentlemen, behold the heart of the last traitor. God save King George.' Upon which the spectators gave a loud huzza. Then he scored each of their arms and legs, but did not cut them off, crying, 'Good people, behold the four quarters of a traitor;' and when he had finished that part of the operation, he chopped off their heads, beginning with Frazier, and ending with Hamilton, which finished the execution."[1] On the next Saturday the remainder of the rebels were executed at the same place.

Two curious facts are recorded with reference to these executions. One is, that in 1754 a tailor, by name William Arundel, assisted by an Irish journeyman, stole from Micklegate Bar the heads of two of the Jacobites, which had been there impaled in 1746. The tailor was fined and imprisoned for two years in the prison upon Ouse Bridge. The second is, that the bodies of those executed were dug up a few years since, by workmen employed in digging a drain behind the Castle. The remains of twenty bodies were found; "but the skulls of three or four of them were wanting, and the bones appeared mixed together in such an unusual manner as to excite the curiosity of all

[1] "Criminal Chronology," p. 61.

who saw the positions in which they were found." The conclusion was that they were the remains of the Scottish rebels executed in 1746, when they were hung, drawn, and quartered.

VICTIMS OF INTOLERANCE, PERSECUTION, AND SUPERSTITION.

CHAPTER VII.

VICTIMS OF INTOLERANCE, PERSECUTION, AND SUPERSTITION.

BLOODTHIRSTY as were the tender mercies of Queen Mary and her advisers, her bigotry was not more cruel than the fierce intolerance of the opposite side. The game, no doubt, was a close one, and Protestantism felt it was on the defensive. But nothing could well justify the savage laws and brutal measures of repression which were enforced when Protestant sovereigns were upon the throne. Under Edward VI. the Roman Catholics were sorely oppressed; not only were their priests sentenced to imprisonment for officiating in their own way, but they were commanded, under the heaviest penalties, to use the new book of liturgy. The people at large were fined whenever they failed to go to church; while all who maintained the Pope's supremacy were deemed guilty of high treason, and sentenced to suffer the tortures recounted in a previous chapter.[1] There had always been in Yorkshire many staunch and steadfast supporters of the old form of faith, crowds of whom in the evil times found themselves among the inmates of York Castle, and the other prisons of the city. "During the reigns of Elizabeth and James I.," says Mr. Raine, "a great number of the Yorkshire Roman Catholics were in prison for their faith. Many of them died in gaol. These were dragged to the service at the Minster, where the Archbishop preached at them, and when his Chaplain, Mr. Bunney, aspersed them from the pulpit with what Anthony A. Woods calls his 'divinity squirt,' they cried out in indignation, and they were actually gagged."[2] Mr. Baring Gould in

---

[1] See ante, p. 107.
[2] Preface to vol. 40, Surtees Society, p. 25.

his "Yorkshire Oddities," gives some of the worst cases on record. That, for instance, of the priest, William Hart, who was sent from Rome to minister to the Yorkshire Catholics, and who, after many narrow escapes when celebrating mass, was captured in bed, and conveyed to York Castle heavily ironed. The dean and superior clergy of York Cathedral strove hard to bring him to conform to the state religion, but "he gently yet firmly refused." Convicted finally of high treason, as well as on the other counts of foreign ordination and performing mass, he was hung, drawn, and quartered. John Amyas and Robert Dalby, priests, from Douay College, sent as missionaries to benighted England, were both taken at York, tried and suffered as traitors. So did old John Lockwood, of good Yorkshire family, who surrendered his succession to his father's property, in order to take orders and brave the dangers of the calling of priest. He spent a lifetime in his perilous mission, and although more than once imprisoned, had reached the advanced age of eighty-seven before he was finally captured and sent to his death. The description of his arrest and removal to York Castle is full of disgusting details, and paints in very sombre colours the ruthless brutality of the law's myrmidons of those days. Another priest, Edmund Catterick, was also in York Castle, and both were tried and sentenced to death. Charles I., with the Prince of Wales, were resident at the Manor House, York, at the time, and the king reprieved the priests, only to sign their death-warrant later on at the strong remonstrance of the Parliament. A more loathsome case was that of Mrs. Clitheroe, who in Elizabeth's reign suffered the penalty of being "pressed to death," for harbouring priests in her house. The Clitheroes' house was a common refuge for them, but at length detection ensued. Mr. Clitheroe escaped, but his wife was taken, lodged in York Castle, and duly arraigned at the Common Hall at York. The manner of her death was repulsively terrible, and a disgrace to the cause which made use of such tortures.[3]

Those whose proclivities were Romish, did not fare well when the Puritans were in power. There were repeated crusades against them. Yet in spite of all, the priests came over in dozens, full of missionary zeal, from the various colleges abroad, where they had been educated and ordained. "It is melancholy," says Raine, "to read the story of these bold and zealous men availing themselves of every device to escape detection, disguising themselves, forging passes, travelling under assumed names, and undergoing every hardship for the sake of their religion." Numbers were arrested, tried, and executed. After the Restoration the fire of persecution for a time slumbered. Yet Roman Catholics were still indicted for not going regularly to the Protestant established churches, a privilege they shared with Nonconformists, Quakers, and other stout-hearted champions

[3] See "Yorkshire Oddities," ii. 240.

of the rights of religious freedom, many of whom, however, were committed to gaol as well for refusing to take the oath of allegiance. But towards the close of Charles the Second's reign, when there were possibilities of a Catholic succession, the Roman Catholics, by their own activity, and the fears their opponents entertained, were subjected to a new oppression.

These were evil times for Roman Catholics. Many seminary priests and Jesuits were apprehended, with the usual fatal consequences to themselves. Thus, as the following deposition, from the fortieth volume of the Surtees Society's publications, shows :—" Upon the 14th August, 1676, before Yorke Horner, Lord Mayor of York, Thomas Thomas sayth, that within twelve dayes past, he see Samuel Banckes, of this city, writing-master, act in the office of a Roman priest within his own house, and that he see him say masse in his owne person, haveinge upon him the robes of a priest, at that tyme before an altar, and that he see the wyne in the sacrament in his hand, severall people, to the number of about seaventeene, beinge then present." December 9, 1678, one John Reeves, of Whitby, being informed that Matthew Lith, of Sleights, being at a wedding, had said, "You talk of Papists and Protestants, but when the roast is ready, I know who shall have the first cutt." Upon which this informer felt himself obliged to search Matthew's house, and states that he did find " a supposed Popish priest there, called Postgate, also Popish books, relicks, wafers, all which said Postgate owned to be his." Postgate stood his trial at the York Assizes, 1679, and was condemned to be hanged, drawn, and quartered, as a Popish priest, which was the sole offence charged. On the 7th August, 1679, he was laid upon a sledge, and drawn through the streets to the place of execution, where the sentence was carried out. His quarters were given to his friends, and interred at York. He was eighty-two years old, had been fifty years a priest in the families of Lady

Hungate, of Saxton, and of Lady Dunbar. One of his hands is preserved as a relic in Douay College. Informers generally received 20*l*. for each conviction. The wretched Reeves never, however, was paid, but, says Challoner, in his Memoirs of the Missionary Priests, "after having suffered for some time an extreme torture in body and mind, was found drowned in a small brook."

Long lists of Roman Catholic recusants in the north are still extant, all of whom were either bound over in sureties or sent to prison. "The most vigorous measures were taken by the executive, and a most virulent persecution commenced, which was fostered with the utmost energies of a few interested and pestilential informers."[4] Several ladies and gentlemen were arrested; two of the Tempests were lodged in York Castle as suspicious characters. This was in connexion with the charge against Sir Thomas Gascoigne, to which reference was made in the preceding chapter. Later on, when

[4] Raine, note to p. 232, Surtees, vol. 40.

the statute of præmunire was put in force, many Roman Catholics who would not take the oath of allegiance were thrown into prison, and otherwise inconvenienced. Raine gives a list of those who were confined in York Castle on this account in July, 1680. Among them were Sir John Lawson, Bart., George Meynell, Esq., Francis Tunstall, Esq., Roger Meynell, Esq., Peter Middleton, Esq., Phillip Constable, Esq., and several ladies. In 1684, both York Castle and the Ouse Bridge Prison had many such inmates. Next year James II. came to the throne. Lists of these sufferers were prepared, no doubt, with the idea of indemnification by the new king, who was a Roman Catholic at heart. The Hon. Mary Fairfax, wife to the Hon. John Fairfax, was one of these; she was a daughter of Colonel Hungate, who was killed fighting for Charles at Chester. "What an outrage," says Raine on this point, "to decency and Christian charity it was, to speak mildly, to confine ladies in a prison which, when the Ouse was high, was partially under water." Another lady prisoner in Ouse Bridge was Magdalen Metham, whose husband's father was killed in Willoughby fight; Catherine Lassells, also, widow to Edward Lassells, "a lieutenant in his late Majesty's service." In York Castle, as shown on the list certified by Sir Thomas Mauleverer and Sir Thomas Rudston, were Francis Ayscough, Esq., who had been a lieutenant in a troop of horse raised by his brother; Ancketillus Bulmer, the son of Anthony Bulmer, lieutenant-colonel in his Majesty's service; and five north-riding gentlemen, Robert Wilson, William Hildred, Robert Berry, Anthony Medcatt, and Edward Burbeck, "all souldiers sequestred and sufferers for their loyalty and service to his late Majesty." There was also Francis Osbaldeston, son of Sir Francis Osbaldeston, "a loyall person, who with imprisonment lyes bed-ridden in the prison near upon these two years, being eighty years old." Anthony Langworth, gent., "whose father was turned out of his estate, whose uncle, Sir John Langworth, ... and his uncle, Sir Francis Prujean, were knighted by his late Majesty. This prisoner is loyall, and a great sufferer in himself and his relations;" also " Simon Nicholson, gent., an Irishman and a stranger, who, travelling through the country, was apprehended and clapt in præmunire." There were several women also imprisoned. Two ladies, Mary and Margarett More, who were living upon a farm in the county, "were committ to præmunire (the said Margarett died in prison)." These Mores, it is stated in the deposition, were lineal descendants of Sir Thomas More, "quondam Lord Chancellor of England." Another lady was Mrs. Mary Wayt, widow of George Wayt, who was lieutenant in Major Markham's troop of horse, "she being of a loyall family of the Lanctons, in Lancashire, whose estate was sold from them for their loyalty, her estate sequestered, for which she is a great sufferer." Rewards and recompenses were no doubt meted out to all these with no stinted hand during the few years that James was in the ascendant, but after the Revolution the waters once more closed over the Catholics, and there are cases again recorded of pains and penalties inflicted upon the priests, although not at York.

Only second in severity to the measures instituted against the Roman Catholics were the penalties under which all suffered who were guilty of breaches against the act of Uniformity. The nonconforming ministers were not only evicted from their livings, but were punished if contumacious by imprisonment. Thus the Rev. Joshua Kirkby, of Wakefield, was sent to York Castle for preaching in his own house. "One of his principal amusements in gaol was writing verses, about which a friendly pen tells us the sense was far beyond the poetry."[5] Great numbers of nonconformists were indicted for not going to church.

Another sect which suffered extremely in

[5] Raine, note to page 97, vol. 40, Surtees Society.

Yorkshire and the north were the Quakers, who only sprang into existence in the later years of the Commonwealth. "The infancy of this religious party was more fiery than its age. The Quakers were concerned more or less in all the plots of the time. It was their delight to abuse the minister in the pulpit, the judge upon the bench. They resisted public order and decency in the grossest manner. They prophesied!! They walked about the streets in the unadorned simplicity of Adam and Eve before they knew *tu quoque*. They howled and bellowed as if an evil spirit was within them." [6] The Yorkshire magistrates clapped all they could lay hold of into York Castle Prison, as poor deluded creatures. Francis Higginson, Vicar of Kirkby Stephen, undertook to vanquish them in print, but he did not succeed. Speaking of the excesses of the Quakers, he says, "The Judges on the Bench they called scarlet-coloured beasts; the Justices—'justices so

[6] Raine, Preface, xxi.

called.' They made it a practice to enter churches with their hats on during divine service, and to rail openly against the ministers, calling them liars, Baal's priests, Babylon's merchants selling beastly ware; bidding them come down from the high places. An amusing instance is related by Raine, in vol. 40, Surtees Society. Mr. Fothergill, Vicar of Orton, one Sunday exchanged duty with Mr. Dalton, of Shap, who had but one eye. A Quaker, stalking as usual into the church of Orton, while Mr. Dalton is preaching, says, "Come down, thou false Fothergill." "Who told thee," says Mr. Dalton, "that my name was Fothergill." "The spirit," quoth the Quaker. "That spirit of thine is a lying spirit," says the other, "for it's well known I am not Fothergill, but Pied Dalton, of Shap!"

Among the depositions we find that the grand jury presented one Mary Fisher, late of Selby, in Yorkshire, for abusing the Rev. Richard Calvert when in his pulpit, with the words "Come downe, come downe, thou painted beast, come downe. Thou art but an hireling, and deludest people with thy lyes." She pleaded guilty and was sentenced to a fine of 200*l*. Again, Elizabeth Hutton was committed in 1652 for "uncivilly reproving" the justices of assize upon the bench, by calling upon them to "come down, thou blynde beasts!" It appeared that the Quakers were punished also for disseminating their opinions, which they sought to do by affixing printed statements on the market crosses and other public places. But it is also clear that although thus summarily dealt with, they were full of vitality, and were not to be easily repressed. They were turbulent, but they had the courage of their convictions, and very frequently endeavoured to force their views upon others, as when a party of them attacked and maltreated the Vicar of Helmsly while he was burying a parishioner.

Very different to the foregoing, but not less to be pitied, were another much ill-used sect or people. The gipsies, or Egyptians, were in those times viewed with something more than suspicion. A Durham record shows that they were hanged for being just what they were. A number of them imprisoned in York Castle in 1649-50, seem to have received treatment only less barbarous than death. They petitioned to William Robinson, Esq., Justice of the Peace in the North Riding, as follows:—" The humble petition of divers distressed persons calling themselves Jepsese. Humbly sheweth, that whereas your worship hath committed us most justly, and according to our deserts to the Castle of York, where wee are, and our poor infants almost famished for want of livelihood. And, much the rayther, by reason the men that by your worship's command brought us hither, did contrary to all equity and Christianity, and as we are informed, contrary to the law of this kingdom, bereft us and tooke from us our mare and many things of greate note and vallew. And without any neede

CLIFFORD'S TOWER—CITY AND CATHEDRAL IN THE DISTANCE.

P

or cause, getting at many townes both meate and money for their own and our use, of which your poor petitioners got smale reliefe. In tender consideration whereof, and soe that your petitioners are most sorry for their former leud course of life, and promiseth by the help of Almighty God will endeavour ourselves to direct our lives hereafter observant to the Will of God and lawes of this land, it therefore would please your worship to commisserate our distressedness, and in your grave wisdom cause the cunstable and others to restore our goods so unjustly tacken from us. And that it would please your worship to call us to the sessions, to receyve such punishment as the worshipfull bench shall think fit, and wee shall be bound to pray." Raine goes on to say that at the assizes all the women pleaded pregnancy before judgment. It was allowed in one case, Barbara Smith, but the others, including Richard Smith, were probably executed.

Still sharper measure had invariably been

meted out to the so-called professors of the black arts. Against witchcraft and sorcery the law had always been most severe. By a statute of Henry VIII., 33, cap. 8, these offences were made felony, without benefit of clergy; and again by statute Jac. I., cap. 12, it was decreed "that all persons invoking any evil spirit, or consulting, or covenanting with, entertaining, employing, feeding, or rewarding any evil spirit; or taking up dead bodies from their graves, to be used in any witchcraft, sorcery, charm, or enchantment; or killing or otherwise hurting any person by such infernal arts; should be guilty of felony without benefit of clergy, and suffer death. And if any person should attempt by sorcery to discover hidden treasures, or to restore stolen goods, or to provoke unlawful love, or to hurt any man or beast, though the same were not effected, he or she should suffer imprisonment and pillory for the first offence, and death for the second.

"These acts continued in force till quite

lately, to the terror of all ancient females in the kingdom, and many poor wretches were sacrificed thereby, to the prejudice of their neighbours and their own illusions; not a few having by some means or other confessed the fact at the gallows."[7]

It was not strange that they should have confessed, when one considers the tortures legally practised in these times. It was asserted that a witch, even when under torture, could only shed three tears, and those out of the left eye; these tears were looked for by the Judges, who then pronounced her guilty. There were two tests by fire—the first by burning the house of the pretended witch; the other by burning any animal supposed to have been bewitched by her. Another test was by water. In swimming a witch, as it was called, she was stripped naked and "cross-bound," the right thumb to the left big toe, and *vice versa;* then thrown into a pond or river, in which, if guilty, she could not

[7] "Blackstone," iv. 209.

sink, for having, by her compact with the devil, renounced the waters of baptism, the waters in turn refused to receive her into their bosom. Inasmuch as it generally happened that when once in the water the witch would be pelted till she either sank or drifted to the bank, the chances were certainly not in her favour. Old women, it was maintained, were generally selected by the spirits of evil for their malicious purposes, who usually appeared to them in the form of a man wearing a black coat or gown; and sometimes, especially in the north, with a "bluish band and turned-up linen cuffs." Hard bargains were sometimes driven between the parties. This was also the case, according to Richard, in the negotiations between Cromwell and the devil before the battle of Worcester. There were black, white, and grey witches. Some were fond of junketing. Satan would often play on a pipe or cittern to make them dance, and not unfrequently he became enamoured of their withered charms, when toads and horrible serpents were the hated progeny of this union. On this point it may be mentioned that Sinclair, in his "Invisible World," tells of a Mr. Barton, who was burnt with his wife for witchcraft. Before being tied to the stake, he confessed (after torture) that he had intrigued with the devil in the shape of a comely lady. His wife confessed at the same time that the devil in the shape of a poodle dog used to dance before her, playing upon the pipes with a candle under his tail. The devil had other amusements, as when further north, particularly in Scotland, he would ever and anon get up into a pulpit and preach a sermon in a voice "hough and gustie." St. Augustine, "Bodin Paracelsus," firmly maintained that the devil was particularly fond of a little flirtation with the ladies. Burton relates the case of a Bavarian widower, who, sadly grieving for his beloved wife, was visited by old Nick, who had assumed the form of the dear departed, and who promised to live with and comfort him on the condition that he " would leave off swearing." He vowed it, married her, and she brought him several children; till one day, in a family quarrel, he swore like a pandour, whereupon she vanished and never more was seen.

The best protection against witchcraft was held to be to take some hair, parings of nails, or any part of a person bewitched, and put them into a stone bottle, with some crooked nails. The whole was then corked close, and hung up the chimney. This expedient, it was said, caused horrible tortures to the witch, until the bottle was uncorked. Witches could not pursue their victims beyond the middle of a running stream, provided the fugitives had been baptized. The belief in witchcraft was the origin of nailing the pad of a fox over a hen-roost, a horseshoe over a stable. The following charm is, in Livonia, held to be a most powerful purge to administer to an evil spirit:—

"Two eyes have seen the ——. May three eyes deign to cast a favourable look upon the

——, in the name of the Father, the Son, and of the Holy Ghost."

The reader is referred to Owen Pike's "History of Crime," vol. i. p. 37, for a full description of the ancient belief in witchcraft. It was supposed that persons subject to epilepsy, mania, or any form of mental weakness, were possessed by a devil, which could be expelled by the performance of certain religious ceremonies. The Church sanctioned a form of exorcism, and the exorcist held the third rank in the ecclesiastical order. In England an attempt was made to combine the forces of medicine with the forces of religion, just as many centuries after, it was the custom to consult a physician upon the cases of persons bewitched (mad). Prescriptions were accordingly given even in those days, not, indeed, for the cure of madness, but for the ejection of devils. The remedies were usually in the form of drinks. Ale was always one of the ingredients, mixed with various herbs.

Sometimes twelve masses were sung over the mixture before it was administered. Sometimes holy water was poured into the ale. One receipt, however, which was considered efficacious against the devil, without any assistance from the Church, was an emetic, which we may suppose dislodged him bodily from his seat in the patient's frame.

Just before the War of the Roses the charge of witchcraft became, like the charge of heresy, a political engine. In the time of child-king Henry VI., after the death of the Duke of Bedford, the Duke of Gloucester was the most powerful person. The chief of the opposition was Cardinal Beaufort, Bishop of Winchester, who had the care and education of the young prince. The clerical party resolved to strike the duke through his wife. She was seized at Leeds, and thrown into prison, afterwards sent to London to take her trial for witchcraft. Her trial took place in St. Stephen's chapel, Westminster. Prelates being the only judges, she was found

VICTIMS OF INTOLERANCE. 223

guilty by the sages of " having, with the assistance of the witch of Eye (Suffolk), made a waxen image of this child-king; of having set it before a fire, so that it might gradually melt away." He did not melt, however, as he was present at her trial, and had sufficient good feeling to save the life her husband's enemies would have taken to spite him. But the fear of torture drove her to admit anything; and in one of the ballads of the day the poor duchess bewails her fate:—

> Through London in many a street
>   Of them that were most principal,
> I went barefoot upon my feet
>   That sometime wont to ride royal.
> Father of Heaven and Lord of all,
>   As Thou wilt so must it be,
> The sign of pride will have a fall,
>   All women may beware of me.

After walking through the streets of London, to be jeered at by a 15th century mob, she was confined in the prison at the Isle of Man. The unfortunate witch of Eye was burnt in Smithfield.

The belief in witchcraft was strong in the north, especially in Northumberland and Yorkshire. There were many strange stories afloat, which credulity and superstition exaggerated, till people trembled at the very name of witch. These wise women, who in our day would have gone into business as spirit-rappers or electro-biologists, had however a large following—from fear, rather than from love. Numbers of silly folk believed in them, and went to them for advice and assistance in trouble. Witches professed to have a knowledge of the healing art, and the gift of second sight, whereby they could recover stolen property. They were to be bribed into complaisance, and could always extort what money they pleased, either by threats, or in return for services rendered. But in return they were liable to be brought before judge and jury at any time, to answer for their misdeeds. "An evil-looking dame meets Mr. Henry Hatefield, of Rhodes, and strikes him on the neck, and his horse also with a docken leave, whereupon the latter sickens and dies, and he himself was very sore troubled, perplexed with a paine in his neck." After which the witch's daughter says to him, " Doth the devil nipp thee in the neck ? but he will nippe you better yet." This witch was committed at the York Assizes. When examined by the women of the village, she was found to bear two witch marks, one behind her ear, the other on her thigh. The daughter of Sir John and Lady Mallory, of Studely Hall, Ripon, was taken seriously ill; lost the use of her limbs, and at times had strange fits. She was always crying, " She comes! she comes!" And, asked who it was, she replied, " Mary, Mary," fixing at last upon one Mary Wade, when many Marys were mentioned to her. "And since the nameing of the said Mary, she hath vomited several strange things, as blotting-paper full of pins and thred about, and likewise a lump of towe with pins and thred tied aboute it, and a piece of wooll and pins in it, and likewise two feathers and a stick." The deposition from which this extract is taken further says that when Mary Wade was brought to Miss Mallory's bedside and confessed her guilt, the young lady immediately recovered. Witches were supposed to be given to all kinds of antics. They rode upon wooden dishes and egg shells; they took the shapes of cats and hares, or, again, of greyhounds or bees. A very curious story is told by Sir John Reresby in his "Memoirs," who gives it as though he was nearly convinced of its truth.[2] The extract is as follows :—" I would venture to take notice of a private occurrence which made some noise at York. The assizes being there held on the 7th March, 1686-87, an old woman was condemned for a witch. Those who were more credulous on points of this nature than myself, conceived the evidence to be very strong against her. The boy she was said to have bewitched, fell down on a sudden before all the Court when he saw her, and would then

[2] Raine, p. xxx

as suddenly return to himself again, and very distinctly relate the several injuries she had done him; but in all this it was observed the boy was free from any distortion; that he did not foam at the mouth, and that his fits did not leave him gradually, but all at once; so that, upon the whole, the judge thought it proper to reprieve her, in which he seemed to act the part of a wise man. But, though such is my own private opinion, I cannot help continuing my story. One of my soldiers being upon guard about eleven in the night, at the gate of Clifford's Tower, the very night after the witch was arraigned, he heard a great noise at the Castle, and, going to the porch, he there saw a scroll of paper creep from under the door, which, as he imagined by the moonshine, turned first into the shape of a monkey, and thence assumed the form of a turkey cock, which passed to and fro by him. Surprised at this, he went to the prison, and called the under-keeper, who came and saw the scroll dance up and down, and creep under the door, where there was scarce an opening of the thickness of half-a-crown. This extraordinary story I had from the mouth of both one and the other; and now leave it to be believed or disbelieved, as the reader may be inclined this way or that."

Much as the persecution of witches is to be reprehended, it is but fair to state that convictions were uncommon, and the infliction of sentences rare. Nor were the credulous of those little enlightened times singular in their belief in witchcraft. Two great authorities may be quoted who confess that they also, in some measure, shared the belief. Addison writes [3] "There are some opinions in which a man should stand neuter, without engaging his assent to one side or the other. It is with this temper of mind that I consider the subject of witchcraft. When I consider whether there are such persons in the world as those we call witches, my mind is divided between the two

[3] "Spectator."

opposed opinions ; or rather, to speak my mind freely, I believe in general that there is, and has been such a thing as witchcraft, but, at the same time, can give no credit to any particular instance of it."

Blackstone, in his Commentaries, quotes Addison, and says for himself, "To deny the possibility, nay, the actual existence of witchcraft and sorcery, is at once flatly to contradict the revealed word of God, in various passages both of New and Old Testament; and the thing itself is a truth to which every nation in the world has in its turn borne testimony, either by example seemingly well attested, or by prohibitory laws which at least suppose the possibility of a converse with evil spirits. The civil law punishes with death not only the sorcerers, but also those who consult them; imitating in the former the express laws of God, ' Thou shalt not suffer a witch to live.' "

A curious story, quoted by Milligan in his "Unlawful Cures," shows that the belief in witchcraft had not disappeared in Yorkshire at a much later date. It is the case of Chief Justice Holt. Everybody nowadays is aware what a powerful agent a medical man has in a patient's belief in his knowledge; especially in nerve diseases, as they may truly be called. A curious anecdote is related of Lord Chief Justice Holt. When a young man, he, with companions, who were law students like himself, ran up a score at an Inn, which they were not able to pay. One of them, Mr. Holt, in fact, observed that the landlord's daughter looked very ill, and, passing himself for a medical student, asked what ailed her, when he was informed she suffered from an ague. Mr. Holt gathered various plants, mixed them with great ceremony, rolled them up in parchment, scrawled some characters on the same, and suspended the roll round the neck of the young woman, and strange to say, the ague did not return. After this cure the doctor offered to pay the bill, to which the grateful landlord would not consent, allowing the party to leave the house. Many years after, when on the Bench, a woman was brought before him, accused of witchcraft, the very last person tried upon such a charge. Her only defence was, that she possessed a ball which never failed to cure the ague. The charm was handed to the judge, who recognized the identical ball with which he had compounded the hotel bill.

NOTORIOUS AND OTHER CRIMINALS.

CHAPTER VIII.

NOTORIOUS AND OTHER CRIMINALS.

THE inmates of York Castle for breaches of the law other than those referred to in the foregoing chapters have represented naturally the crimes from time to time most prevalent in Yorkshire and the North. Some among them doubtless achieved an unenviable notoriety, but the greater number were for the most part but commonplace criminals. Authentic records for the earlier ages are not forthcoming. Raine, speaking of the seventeenth century, speaks rather favourably of that period in regard to crime. "Murders," he says, "were less numerous than might have been expected. Rape was almost unknown. There were, however, robbers of almost every description, from the famous Nevison to the ordinary cut-purse. Horse-stealing was a very frequent offence,[1] especially in the time of the civil wars, and among the disbanded soldiery. Cattle-stealing, which is now so rare, was one of the common vices both of town and country. But perhaps the most serious and frequent crime was the clipping and the deterioration of coin. No one can have an idea of the extent to which this infamous trade was carried on."[2] In one instance the offence was actually brought home to a clergyman, the rector of the parish of Bothal, near Morpeth—the Rev. John Booth. The case was clearly proved; a workman deposes to have built him a fire-hearth; another

---

[1] A good story is told which bears upon this offence in Yorkshire. A Yorkshire man and a man of Lincolnshire were once disputing as to the relative fertility of the two countries. "In Lincolnshire," said the one, "if you put a horse in a field over night you won't see his legs in the morning, the grass will have grown so high." "In Yorkshire," says the other, "you may put a horse in a field over night and you won't see him at all in the morning."

[2] Raine, Preface, p. xvi.

that the parson borrowed a pair of bellows from the village smith; a third, a Newcastle goldsmith, states that he purchased from Booth nine hundred ounces of "rund" silver and bullion. Booth fled for his life—the punishment was capital—and does not appear to have been apprehended.

Another clipping case, three years later, appears in these same depositions from York Castle. Daniel Auty, of Dewsbury, showed an informant "foureteene ounces of bullion, which he confest he had clipt, and he exchanged part of itt with this informant for 2 silver spoones." Other deponents swore to other quantities of bullion received from Auty, who, with all his kith and kin, are said to have been adepts in dishonest practices. The village of Dewsbury enjoyed a very evil reputation in those days. This Auty was afterwards in gaol at York Castle for sacrilege. The communion plate of York Minster had been stolen, and he with his sister were charged with, but not convicted of, the crime. Yet there was a witness who deposed, but on hearsay evidence, that the plate had been seen in a house in Dewsbury, when Auty and his brother were present, and that it was melted down in the same house. Lockwood, another witness, who, Raine says, was at one time gaoler of York Castle, deposed that Auty had told him that he (Auty), with several prisoners in York Castle, had been discoursing about the Minster plate, and "what a rare booty it would be if it could bee gott." Lockwood was at the time servant to Lady Beaumont, in Lord Irwin's house, a plain proof that he was not of a very high class in life, and that, if he held it, the office of gaoler of York Castle, could not then have been of any high esteem.

Cases of coining counterfeit money were not infrequent, and were dealt with as severely as clipping, being punishable with death. The earliest record of an execution at York for this offence is that of Frederic Gottfried and Thomas Carrat, one of Hull, the other of Keswick, but evidently of foreign extraction, who suffered on the gallows of St. Leonard's Green Dykes, for "coining guineas in Thursday Market, in the city of York." Another case, that of George Foster, occurred in 1582, when ten thousand persons viewed the ceremony. There were four other cases before the end of the century, and another batch of four, two men and two women, were similarly punished in 1602, "for counterfeiting the good coin of this realm called guineas."

Highway robbery was, however, as fruitful a source of supply as any for both prison and gallows. According to the Criminal Chronology of York Castle," the first recorded case of execution for this offence, is that of Henry William Genyembre, who, although a man advanced in years, was guilty of robbery upon the king's highway, as well as horse-stealing. This was in 1585. Five years later two others were also executed for the same offence, committed on the Hull road, near Rexby. The manner in which such a robbery was carried out is shown in the deposition of the Earl of Dumfries, who, returning from the south with his servants, was attacked and robbed between Lincoln and Bawtry. He deposed himself that, "beinge ridinge on the high road betwixte Lincolne and Doncaster, he was sett upon by Nicholas Spavild and Richard Drew, on the 26th November, who took from him one bay mare and a black nagg, with a great lether mail full of goods. Thereupon hee was forced to goe to Bawtry on foote, and there raysed the hue and crye after them." They were caught, and their defence was that the gentleman was riding off the road over the corn; when they remonstrated, he (Lord Dumfries) and his servant dismounted and walked away, leaving the horses, which they took to the pinfold or pound. On another occasion a clothier was stopped in the broad daylight, about ten in the forenoon, on Killinghall Moor, on his way to Ripon, by three persons, one of whom clapped a pistol to his breast and bade him deliver. His pockets were searched, and fourteen shillings taken out. Another of the robbers cut the " wametow," and, taking the packs off the driven horse, searched them and extracted forty pounds, which were given to one of the party, Thomas Lightfoot. This Lightfoot was a Quaker who had recently escaped from Durham Gaol. Lightfoot was also charged with having searched the clothier's daughter, Sarah, in a very rude and uncivil fashion, and did take out of her pocket a little box, wherein there was a shilling and threepence.

Amos Lawson, many years later, was a most noted highwayman, whose daring exploits gained him great notoriety. He long continued his outrages unchecked, but was arrested at length, in 1644, in the forest of Galtres, by William Taylor, who was then sheriff of the city of York, and whom he had intended to rob. Ebenezer Moor was another most notorious and intrepid highwayman, whom retribution did not overtake till he had planned and executed many daring robberies. William Nevison was, however, the most celebrated of that century.

Nevison will be interesting to the general reader as the person who really performed that with which fiction, as rendered by William Harrison Ainsworth in his "Rookwood," has credited Dick Turpin. The latter's ride to York was never authenticated, but there are good grounds for supposing that Nevison did actually accomplish the feat of riding from London to York in one day, in May, 1684. There were many points of difference between these two noted highwaymen. Both were, no doubt, desperate fillibusters; but while Turpin (of whom more later) was clearly a braggart, a bully, and a cowardly murderer, nothing of the kind could be alleged against Nevison. He was a man of pleasing address, of large stature, of gentlemanly manners, and unparalleled courage. "Nevison," says Raine, "may be appropriately called the Claude Duval of the North. The chroniclers of his deeds have told us of his daring and his charities, for he gave away to the poor much of the money he took from the rich." Once, as the History of York tells us, he was at a village public-house, when the talk turned upon a poor farmer, who had been sold up by the bailiffs. The bailiff with the cash upon him was actually at the public-house at the same time. Nevison determined to rob him of it, which he effected by pretending to retire to bed, but descending from the window to the road, he lay in wait for the bailiff, and presently eased him of the cash. Returning to his lodgings through the window, he passed a good night, and proceeded next morning to the farmer's, whose heart he gladdened by restoring him, to the last penny, the price of the farm. Nevison, it was said, only borrowed from the poor; if he robbed them, that is to say, he restored them their money when he had made a good haul from the rich. He was so terrible to the carriers and drovers of the north, that they paid him black mail in the shape of a quarterly contribution, which secured them from himself, and obtained his powerful protection against other knights of the road.

He appears to have been arrested and in custody in March, 1676, but the depositions are too imperfect to gather from them the nature of the offence with which he was charged. He was, however, condemned, "but was reprieved, together with a woman named Jane Nelson, in the expectation that he would discover his accomplices. The hope was a vain one, and he was draughted into a regiment destined for Tangiers, from which he quickly deserted, and resumed his old career."[3] He was next captured near Wakefield, charged with a series of crimes, of which he was convicted, and sentenced to be hanged, but he managed to break out of prison, and again took to the road, to be at last captured by a Captain Hardcastle, who arrested him (for a trifling robbery in a public-house, near Sandal) at the town of Milford. He was

[3] Raine, note, p. 220, Surtees Society, vol. 40.

sent to York Castle and hanged on the gallows over against Knavesmire, out Micklegate Bar, May 4th, 1684. Mary Burton, in her deposition, stated that the gang for whom she was housekeeper, consisted of Edmond Bracy, of Nottingham; John Nevison, of York; Thomas Wilbore, Nottingham; Thomas Tankard, Lincolnshire; John Bromett; William or Robert Iverson, of no certain abode, but commonly at the "Talbott," in Newarke. The "Talbott" was their head-quarters, where they divided their spoil. At this Inn they kept rooms by the year. She connected them with ten great robberies, by which they realized 1500*l.* of money as valued at that date. "She thinks the master of the 'Talbott' is privy to their carriages, for that shee hath often seene them whisper together; as alsoe one William Anwood, the ostler there, shee havinge often seene the said partyes give him good summs of money, and order him to keepe their horses close, and never to water them but in the night time."

These men, naturally, frequented fairs, races, &c., and of course had receiving-houses in different parts of the country. This put them at the mercy of the receivers, whom they were obliged to conciliate with gifts, which leads to the trite remark that then, as now, receivers are indispensable to act ve criminals, and while running much less risk really make greater gains and merit greater blame.

According to "Bloody news from Yorkshire, or the great robbery committed by twenty highwaymen upon fifteen butchers, as they were riding to Northallerton Fair," (4°., London, 1674,) and a letter written by one George Skipwith, of Howden, who appears to have had betting transactions with the gang, or more probably, to have been a receiver, it appears that John Nevison's real name was John Brace, or Bracy, that he originally belonged to Agnes-Burton, having an uncle thereabouts, and that he was married, his wife living beyond Pontefract. However, he was like a sailor, for he had a wife in every port. Brace, Bracy, or Nevison, chiefly worked in Yorkshire. The gang appear only to have united for grand operations, though their profits appear to have been conducted on the co-operative system. But Nevison was the leader and the most famous. His name and deeds were long sung in local doggrel; witness the following :—

> Did you ever hear tell of that hero,
>   Bold Nevison, that was his name?
> He rode about like a bold hero,
>   And with that he gain'd great fame.
>
> He maintain'd himself like a gentleman,
>   Besides he was good to the poor,
> He rode about like a bold hero,
>   And he gain'd himself favour therefore.
>   *Old Ballad.*

The date of his ride from London to York cannot be exactly fixed. It must have been in the summer, when the days were long, and was probably just previous to the date of his arrest and trial in 1676. The story goes that he had committed a robbery in London just before dawn, and being recognized he jumped on his horse and made for the north. By sunset—that is to say, in fifteen hours, taking the sun's rise at 4 a.m. and its setting at 7 p.m.—he entered York, having ridden the same mare just 200 measured miles. He was afterwards captured there, but could prove a nearly unanswerable alibi. It was shown on his trial that he was seen on the bowling-green at York on the evening of the day the robbery was committed in London. The London witnesses swore positively to him, but neither Judge nor jury would believe them, and Nevison was acquitted. Charles II. christened him "Swift Nick." He was never charged with murder—only with attempting it; and the only occasion on which he shed blood was when a butcher with some half-dozen people were bent upon his capture, and he had to use his pistols in self-defence, and the butcher suffered.

Turpin was a much greater rascal than Nevison, having been in turn highwayman,

The condemned cell in which Nevison and Turpin spent their last days. Shrift was short in those days between sentence and execution.

horse-stealer, and murderer. He was eventually hanged at York, April 17th, 1739. He was the son of a farmer residing at Thackstead, in Essex, in which village he received such education as was likely to be given in that day by the village schoolmaster, who afterwards became the postmaster. Turpin was apprenticed to a butcher in Whitechapel, and was always noted for his rowdy habits and brutal manners. Coming out of his apprenticeship, he set up for himself by marrying a girl named Palmer, of East Ham, Essex, and stealing cattle, for sale elsewhere; this was about 1730. When Essex got too hot, he shifted to Middlesex and Kent, formed a gang, committing murder and robbery in all directions. His turn of mind went more towards seating old women on their own fires, than meeting men in open fight. He was rather a low type of animal, not prepossessing in appearance, and much marked with small-pox. After unintentionally shooting King, his comrade, and the better man of the two, Turpin hid himself in Lincolnshire, taking his wife's name of Palmer, and continuing his old trades, but chiefly that of cattle-lifting. Arrested at last, he escaped from the police, and settled himself at Welton, near Beverley, as Mr. Palmer, a gentleman horse-dealer, a sure introduction to sporting circles. He seems, for some time, to have acted his part well, gaining favour with all who wanted to buy a good horse at a decent price. These he could sell cheap, because he "borrowed" from Lincolnshire. By this conduct he became recognized in a kindly way in the hunting-field, and often went shooting with people of good position. But bad blood will out. Returning from such a party one day, after a poor day's sport, he wantonly shot a cock belonging to his landlord. One Mr. Hall told him, "It was a shame," upon which Mr. Palmer said, "He would shoot him too, if he would wait till he (Turpin) loaded the gun." This line of folly naturally led to a summons at Beverley Petty

Sessions, when being ordered to find bail and sureties, it appeared he "had no friends," so he was committed to Beverley Bridewell. On re-examination he admitted having lived at Long Sutton in Lincolnshire, and on inquiry there soon appeared some fifty people who wanted Palmer, "on which the Beverley magistrates thought it 'prudent' to send him to York Castle." From thence he wrote to his brother at Thackstead, Essex, to "cook" him a good character, but unfortunately for him the handwriting was not recognized, and his brother preferred to keep the postage, sixpence; so the letter went back as a dead letter to the village postmaster his former teacher. Looking at the address he recognized the hand as that of Turpin, whom he had taught to write, and whom he knew had been greatly "wanted" for many years. This Mr. Smith, the postmaster, went to York, and identified him at once as Turpin from among all the prisoners in York Castle. He was seen later on by another, who pretended to know him well; but this man said "that he was not Turpin, and would bet half-a-guinea on it;" on which Turpin whispered to his warder, "Lay him! I'll go you halves."

His demeanour at his execution has already been described.[4] But although the account declares he was distinguished by the comeliness of his appearance, it is difficult to understand the grounds on which this favourable opinion was based. He was not at all prepossessing, really having high, broad cheekbones, a short visage, the face narrowing towards the chin, and was much marked by the small-pox. After execution the corpse was taken by the "mourners" to the "Blue Boar," in Castlegate; they then buried it in the churchyard of St. George's parish. Some enterprising surgeons dug him up, but the populace, ascertaining where he had been taken, fetched him out of a garden at the back of Stonegate, and carried the body in a sort of procession through

[4] See ante, p. 110.

the streets, eventually replacing it in the grave. The leg-irons, said to have been worn by Turpin, are as likely as not to have been worn by Nevison and other prisoners. They weigh 28lbs., and may be now seen in the York Museum.

As to Nevison's own personal strength, and the mare's power of endurance, which enabled them to perform a journey of 200 miles in a day of fifteen hours (or about thirteen miles an hour including halts), the man's feat was equalled by that of John Lepton of York, Esquire to James I., who, for a wager, undertook to ride on six consecutive days between London and York, and performed it accordingly. He first set out from Aldersgate, May 20th, 1606, and accomplished the journey every day before it was dark, "to the greater praise of his strength in acting, than to his discretion in undertaking it."[5] Of course he rode a fresh animal every day, and there is nothing to show he did not change every ten miles. Lepton selected the

[5] Fuller's "Worthies."

period of the year near to the longest day, and fortune similarly favoured Nevison, the former riding 20th to 26th May, the latter probably in the same month some sixty odd years afterwards. It is curious that both these rides took place during the month of May; that Nevison was executed in the month of May, and Turpin in April, with fifty years more or less between them.

    Lepton's ride, May 20th . . . 1606.
    Nevison's ride, about May . . 1684.
    Turpin executed, April 17 . . 1734.

Although murders were not so numerous as might have been expected in the seventeenth century they were not infrequent; nor did they miss certain barbarous features worthy almost of this present enlightened age, when maid-servants brain and then boil their mistresses, and husbands and brothers combine to torture a half-witted wife to death. The cruel wretch Elizabeth Coot, who killed her mother in 1605 by burning her to death; the two young girls, who, in 1647, deliberately poisoned their sweethearts by putting oxalic acid into their drink at the sign of the " Maypole," Clifton ; William Vasey, who drowned Marian, the housekeeper of Mr. Earle, of Beningborough Hall ; Mary Cotnam, who murdered her own daughter; Captain Bolton, an officer, who strangled his maid-servant and buried her in a cellar, all of whom suffered at York, are but typical cases of numbers that have happened since. There is nothing new in the details of the murder of the yeoman Fletcher, of Raskelfe, by his wife and her lover Ralph Raynard. The two wretches had intrigued together before marriage, and then conspired to get Fletcher out of the way. One Mark Dunn, of Huby, assisted, and the three drowned Fletcher as he crossed Dawnay Bridge, on the road over the Lund to Raskelfe. Fletcher's wife had lain in ambush close by with a sack, in which the corpse was to be conveyed to Raynard's garden, or croft, where it was buried, and mustard seed sown in the place. Fletcher had, however, before the murder, addressed a note to his sister, containing the following doggrel:—

"If I should be missing or suddenly in wanting be, mark Ralph Raynard, mark Dunn, and my own wife for me." Then, so the story goes, the ghost of the murdered man appeared to Raynard in a stable at Topcliffe Fair, and said to him, " Ralph, Ralph, repent, for my vengeance is at hand," and ever after the ghost seemed to stand over him. Raynard was so disconcerted, that he at length confessed, and all three were thereupon arrested, convicted, and hanged at the York Tyburn. The woman does not appear to have been burnt after hanging, as was common in cases of petty treason, but all three bodies were hanged in chains on the road near where the murder had been committed.

But among the murders recorded in Yorkshire are some of rather unusual character, both from the rank and position of the culprits, and, in one or two cases, the atrocity with which they were committed. The depositions already frequently quoted, describe how Mr. Wortley, a hot-blooded gentleman, practising as an attorney, resenting the interference of bailiffs coming to arrest him, violently resisted them. " I arrest you," says the bailiff, " at the suit of the Queen Mother." " I will run you through," he replied ; " thou shalt arrest none of me." Then trying to escape, and being prevented, he makes two passes at the bailiff with a rapier, and at the second pass runs him through the body. Mr. Wortley was tried for this, but acquitted. Blood was spilt often enough in turbulent brawls, and fatal duels are on record, in which the survivors were brought to justice, but seldom punished for what they had done. The most notorious case of this kind was that of the Earl of Eglinton, who killed a Mr. Maddox, at the Angell Inn, Doncaster, after a quarrel over the dice. There was a long affray, during which Mr. Maddox, in defending himself against Lord Eglinton, who had drawn his rapier, seized his lordship by the perriwig. My lord then cried with an oath, "I will kill you," and shortened his sword. A bystander, striving vainly to keep the peace, struck up the sword. In the end Lord Eglinton wounded Mr. Maddox in the left side; and, on examination of the body, it was found that the dead man was wounded also in the thigh. Lord Eglinton was tried for his life at York, found guilty, and sentenced to death. But he was reprieved till the king's pleasure was known, and subsequently allowed to go at large. This was in 1681.

But by far the most terrible tragedy of its kind had happened in the early part of that century at Calverly Park, the same place as that where the lodge-keeper was killed last year (1879) by D'Arcy, who suffered death for it at York. The perpetrator of the crime was the head of the family, Walter Calverly, or Calverly of Calverly, as he was commonly called, and it was so atrocious that it would in modern times have probably been explained on the ground of temporary insanity, and its perpetrator would have spent the remainder of his days incarcerated "during her Majesty's pleasure," instead of dying upon the gallows. It was a domestic crime; one which equals in horror the most terrible of its kind. A dramatic story, called the Yorkshire Tragedy, which has been attributed to Shakespeare, was founded upon its incidents. The chief actor in this awful affair was a gentleman of good birth and position, with an assured income from his estates and a fine manor house, part of which is still standing. He was spoken of in his youth as accomplished, and of "a grave, silent, and apparently solid manner." It was thought by most that he would be a credit to his ancestors, and an honour to his country. There were some unbiassed observers, however, who "seem to have considered him deficient in candour and frankness, if they did not actually suspect him of hypocrisy." He began life by falling desperately in love with a young lady, whom, when betrothed to her, he jilted for a new and fairer face. His bride was Miss Philippa Brooke, whom he married in hot haste in London, and took with him to Calverly Hall. Very soon, however, he tired of the pure joys of a country life; wearied of his wife, and sought excitement by " the unlimited gratification of his desires." .... He plunged into excesses of all kinds, mortgaged part of his estates, incurred debts; and, finally, when his own name had sunk so low in worldly estimation that it would no longer obtain him credit, involved a number of his best friends in his difficulties. " His wife, tender and loving through all, sought to wean him from his evil ways, to soothe him in his troubles, and to smoothe difficulties from his path. She even surrendered her jewels to him that he might raise money on them, and finally promised him to sell her dowry, which consisted of landed property, starting for London from Calverly with that express intention. During her absence her husband relapsed rapidly into dissipation, and as he sank deeper and deeper into vice, became so lost to all sense of decency, that he was taken to task for his vile abuse of his own absent wife, and fought a duel with a neighbour who defended her. Now by degrees there settled upon him a growing dislike for her and his children, which deepened ere long into violent hatred. Upon his wife's return without the money from the dowry, which had, however, been promised by her uncle, Calverly's fury broke out in a wild paroxysm, and he threatened to murder her then and there. The announcement that an old college friend had called saved Mrs. Calverly for the moment, but this visit was the cause of all the woes that followed. The friend had called to say that Calverly's younger brother had been thrown into prison; he had been security for Calverly in a bond for a thousand pounds, which was now forfeited, and unless Calverly forthwith paid up the sum, the young man would be ruined for life. Goaded to madness by this demand, Calverly's rage passed all bounds. Dismissing his visitor, he rushed up to a gallery, where he found his eldest child at play. To stab him to the heart with a dagger was his first act. He then rushed to his wife's room, carrying the dead child in his arms. His wife lay asleep. A maid who was with her, nursing the younger child, aghast at the sight of her master covered with blood, was on the point of rousing her mistress, when Calverly rushed at the girl, and threw her downstairs. He next stabbed his second child, who fell moaning on the floor. The poor wife, now awake, and taking in the whole terrible situation, threw herself upon her husband to try and save the child's life. But she only received several wounds herself, and was left for dead by Calverly, who now remembered he had another child at a house two miles distant, and hastened away to kill it too.

As he descended the stairs a man-servant

met him, with the words, "Oh, sir! what have you done?" "That which you will never live to see me repent of!" replied the monster, as he aimed a blow at the man with his dagger. But the servant closed with his master, and the two rolled over together. Calverly, however, tore the man so much with his spurs that he got the best of the struggle, and evading the servant's grasp, he rose to his feet and hurried to the stables to saddle a horse. On his way he met the college friend, who had not left the house, who accosted him, saying he hoped nothing unpleasant had occurred.

"Oh, that," cried Calverly, "is as men shall see and understand things; for look you, sir, what shall make some laugh, shall make others weep, and again, that which some shall deem well and wisely done, shall to others be as a sin and a stumbling-block," and he pressed on, mounted a horse, and galloped off.

When, however, the friend had entered the house, he realized fully all the horrors of the situation, and rising to the emergency, declared that Calverly must at once be pursued. They might never have overtaken him. But providentially, while following his headlong course, his horse had stumbled, and Calverly was thrown. The horse galloped off without him, and the man, bruised and hurt, was compelled to move forward on foot. This gave his pursuers time to come up, and he was presently captured and taken before Sir John Howley, a magistrate for the West Riding. During his examination he preserved a sullen demeanour, it is said. But afterwards he requested an interview with his wife, who had just escaped with her life. "What occurred at this interview it is impossible at this date to discover. From this time forth, however, the murderer seems to have been a softened and a sane man." He was tried at York, but on arraignment refused to plead. The penalty of standing mute was under the existing barbarous code, the sentence of *peine forte et dure*. The judge reminded the prisoner of this, to which Calverly replied,—

"I am familiar with everything you can urge, my lord, I know full well that I shall die under lingering tortures, ... but such pains are welcome to me; they are the only atonement I can offer to man or heaven."

The terrible sentence of pressing to death was accordingly passed upon him, and he endured his punishment on the 5th August, 1604. The manner of inflicting death by pressing was very horrible. The unfortunate malefactor having been stripped, was laid with his back on a board, on which was a sharp stone, sometimes a sharp spike. This entered the spine, then weights were piled on till the ribs were broken, and life was extinct.

Another criminal, with whose name all readers of English literature must be familiar, was closely connected with York Castle. Eugene Aram was by birth a Yorkshireman; he came of good family, which had, however, declined in prosperity, so that Aram's father was employed as gardener by Sir Edward Blackett. The young Aram exhibited early that remarkable taste for learning which subsequently gained him an honourable name, and his precocious tastes were fostered by his father's master. By sixteen, Aram had already acquired much erudition, which he increased from year to year, mastering not only Latin and Greek, but Hebrew also, with extraordinary speed and ease. To these, while engaged as usher or tutor in various parts of the kingdom, he added Chaldaic and Arabic, with botany, heraldry, and many of the sciences. He was living, married, at Knaresborough, in Yorkshire, from 1743, where a Mr. William Norton was his patron, and afforded him the assistance necessary for the pursuit of his studies. But while thus engaged, Aram appears to have fallen in with evil associates. He became especially intimate with one Houseman, a flax-dresser, and the two entered into a confederacy with another man, Clarke, who was to borrow plate and other valuables from his friends, and defraud them of them. Clarke was enabled to do this on the credit of a reputed fortune, which was to come to him with his wife; but he bought also, and pretended in this respect to act as agent for a London merchant, who wished to send the goods abroad.

Suddenly Clarke disappeared, and was heard of no more. Aram and Houseman, who had been his associates, were suspected of complicity in the fraud, but although the houses of both were searched, little was found to incriminate them. A little later Aram also left Knaresborough, and nothing more was heard of him till he was found thirteen years afterwards an usher in a school at Lynn. Nothing more would have been heard of Clarke had not a labourer discovered, when digging at a place called Thistle Hill, near Knaresborough, the skeleton of a body, which had evidently been buried double, and which pointed clearly to some foul play. Suspicion arose that this skeleton was that of Daniel Clarke, and it was now remembered that Aram's wife—whom he had deserted—had hinted years before that her husband and Houseman had made away with Clarke. Search was made for Houseman. He was found, turned king's evidence, and directly accused Aram of the murder. His story went that he and Aram had left the house of the latter in company with Clarke, and that on reaching a place called St. Robert's Cave, Houseman saw Aram strike Clarke "several times over the breast and head, and saw him fall as if he was dead, upon which he came away and left them." He added later that Clarke's body was buried in the cave, where, in effect, it was subsequently found.

An inquiry was now set on foot for Aram, who was eventually found at Lynn. He was questioned, but denied that he had ever been at Knaresborough, or that he had ever known a man named Daniel Clarke. John Barker, a constable of Knaresborough, identified him, and he was apprehended and conveyed to York Castle, where he was tried in August, 1759.

In his defence he argued so ably, and with so much specious cleverness, that the judge characterized his speech as one of the most ingenious pieces of reasoning which had ever fallen under his notice. He pleaded first his known studious habits, and his hitherto unblemished life. " My days," he said, " were honestly laborious ; my nights intensely studious." He urged that Clarke's disappearance was no proof that he was dead, and he quoted the case of the prisoner Thompson, who had escaped two years previously from York Castle,[6] and of whom nothing more had been heard. He pointed out that human bones were so constantly discovered, that there could be nothing extraordinary in the appearance of these in St. Robert's Cave. Lastly, he deprecated the acceptance of circumstantial evidence and king's evidence, quoting many instances where both had been subsequently proved utterly false.

[6] See ante, p. 147.

Nevertheless he was found guilty, and was sentenced to death. After his conviction he acknowledged the justice of his sentence, and confessed to the clergyman who ministered to him that he had actually murdered Clarke. His excuse was that he suspected Clarke of having intrigued with Mrs. Aram. Bulwer, in his novel, " Eugene Aram," which, though one of his masterpieces, gives a fictitious interest to Aram's character, by investing it with many fine traits, makes his hero declare that he was led to murder Clarke, in the hope of obtaining money to carry out some great scientific discovery. The novelist deals as he pleases with his story; but the facts of the case clearly show that Aram was solely influenced by greed.

Aram was executed at the Tyburn, York, but he nearly cheated the gallows. The morning of the execution, when roused to have his irons removed, he was found too weak to rise. On examination it was discovered that he had opened a vein in his arm, with a razor which he had concealed in his cell. He was, however, promptly tended and so far restored, that he stood the journey to Knavesmire, and there met his end. After execution his body was hung in chains in Knaresborough Forest.

A paper was found in his cell, written, as it was supposed, just before he cut his arm with the razor. It was a rhapsodical excuse for his attempted suicide, and ended as follows:—

"I slept soundly till three o'clock, awaked, and then wrote these lines:—

> "Come, pleasing rest, eternal slumber fall,
> Seal mine that once must seal the eyes of all;
> Calm and composed my soul her journey takes,
> No guilt that troubles, and no heart that aches.
> Adieu! thou sun, all bright like her arise;
> Adieu! fair friends, and all that's good and wise."

Execution behind York Castle in the olden time.—From "Drake's History"

LONDON :
GILBERT AND RIVINGTON, PRINTERS,
ST. JOHN'S SQUARE.

A CATALOGUE OF

NEW & POPULAR WORKS,

AND OF BOOKS

FOR CHILDREN,

SUITABLE FOR PRESENTS AND SCHOOL PRIZES.

PUBLISHED BY

GRIFFITH AND FARRAN,

(SUCCESSORS TO NEWBERY AND HARRIS),

WEST CORNER OF ST. PAUL'S CHURCHYARD, LONDON.

E. P. DUTTON AND CO., NEW YORK.

18M. 9.79.   *Cancelling all previous Editions of this Catalogue.*

CONTENTS.

	PAGE
New Books and New Editions, 1879—80	3
New Fiction	4
Standard Works	5
Stanesby's Illuminated Gift Books	7
Poetry	8
Birthday Books...	8
Manuals on Confirmation, &c.	8
New Books and New Editions for Children	9
Six Shilling Books	12
Five Shilling Books	12
Four and Sixpenny Books	14
Three and Sixpenny Books	15
Three Shilling Books	19
Two and Sixpenny Books	20
Two Shilling Books	23
One and Sixpenny Books	24
One Shilling Books	26
The Favourite Library	26
Durable Nursery Books	27
Works for Distribution	28
Educational Works	29

NEW BOOKS AND NEW EDITIONS.

TRAVEL, WAR, AND SHIPWRECK. By Captain W. Parker Gillmore ("Ubique,") Author of "The Great Thirst Land," &c. Demy 8vo. 9s.

POLITICIANS OF TO-DAY. A Series of Personal Sketches. By T. Wemyss Reid, Author of "Charlotte Brontë; a Monograph." Cabinet Portraits, &c. Crown 8vo.

RECORDS OF YORK CASTLE, FORTress, Court House, and Prison. By A. W. Twyford (the present Governor) and Major Arthur Griffiths, author of "The Memorials of Millbank." Crown 8vo. With Engravings and Photographs. 7s. 6d.

L'ABÉCÉDAIRE OF FRENCH PRONUNciation. A Manual for Teachers and Students. By G. Le Prevost, of Paris, Professor of Languages. Crown 8vo.

THE BIRTHDAY BOOK OF QUOTATIONS and Autograph Album. Extracts in English, French, and German, chiefly from standard authors. With Calendar, Ornamental Borders for Photographs, Album for Translations, and Chosen Mottoes. Extra cloth and gilt, price 10s. 6d.

FIFTY YEARS IN SANDBOURNE. A Sketch by Cecilia Lushington. Fcap. 8vo.

AMBITION'S DREAM. A Poem in two fyttes. New Edition. Fcap. 8vo.

THE ROYAL UMBRELLA. By Major A. F. P. Harcourt, author of "The Shakespeare Argosy," &c., &c. With four full-page Illustrations by Linley Sambourne. Small crown 8vo.

CREWEL WORK. Fifteen designs in Bold and Conventional Character, capable of being quickly and easily worked. With complete instructions. By Zeta, Author of "Ladies Work and How to Sell it," and including Patterns for Counterpanes, Bed Hangings, Curtains, Furniture Covers, Chimney-piece Borders, Piano Backs, Table Cloths, Table Covers, &c., &c. Demy, price 2s. 6d.

NEW FICTION.

WON FROM THE WAVES: or, the Story of MAIDEN MAY. By W. H. G. KINGSTON. Three Volumes. Crown 8vo, 31s. 6d.

WORTHLESS LAURELS. By EMILY CARBINGTON. Three volumes crown 8vo. 31s. 6d.

LOUIS: or, Doomed to the Cloister. A Tale of Religious Life in the time of Louis XIV. Founded on Fact. By M. J. HOPE. Dedicated by permission to Dean Stanley. Three volumes, crown 8vo., 31s. 6d.

TRIED BY FIRE. By FRANCIS CARR, Author of "Left Alone," "Not Lancelot Nor Another," &c. Three vols., Crown 8vo., 31s. 6d.

FOR A DREAM'S SAKE. By Mrs. HERBERT MARTIN, Author of "Bonnie Lesley," &c. Two vols., Crown 8vo., cloth, 21s.

THE SECRET OF THE SANDS; or, The Water Lily and her Crew. A Nautical Novel. By HARRY COLLINGWOOD. Two vols., Crown 8vo., cloth, gilt tops, price 12s.

STORIES FOR DAUGHTERS AT HOME.

STEPHEN THE SCHOOLMASTER. A story without plot. By M. E. B. (Mrs. GELLIE). Cr. 8vo., 5s.

MY SISTER'S KEEPER: A Story for Girls. In one vol. By LAURA M. LANE, Author of "Gentleman Verschoylo," &c. With a Preface by Mrs. TOWNSEND, President of the Girls' Friendly Society. Cloth, price 5s.

MY MOTHER'S DIAMONDS; A Domestic Story for Daughters at Home. By MARIA J. GREER. With a Frontispiece by A. LUDOVICI. Cloth, price 5s.

"BONNIE LESLEY:" A Novelette in One Volume. By Mrs. HERBERT MARTIN, Author of "Cast Adrift, &c." With Frontispiece by Miss C. PATERSON. Cloth, price 5s.

LEFT ALONE; or, The Fortunes of Phillis Maitland. By FRANCIS CARR, Author of "Not Lancelot, nor another," &c. Cloth, price 5s.

ST. NICHOLAS' EVE and other Tales. By MARY C. ROWSELL. Crown 8vo. Price 7s. 6d.

PICTURES OF THE PAST: Memories of Men I Have Met, and Sights I Have Seen. By FRANCIS H. GRUNDY, C.E. One vol., Crown 8vo., cloth., price 12s.

Contains personal recollections of Patrick Branwell Brontë, Leigh Hunt and his family, George Henry Lewes, George Parker Bidder, George Stephenson, and many other celebrities, and gives besides descriptions of very varied experiences in Australia.

AMONG THE ZULUS: The Adventures of Hans Sterk in South Africa. By Lieut.-Col. A. W. DRAYSON, R.A. Crown 8vo., illustrated, paper boards, price 2s. 6d.; cloth, gilt edges, price 3s. 6d.

STORIES from EARLY ENGLISH LITERATURE, with some Account of the Origin of Fairy Tales, Legends and Traditionary Lore. Adapted to the use of Young Students. By Miss S. J. VENABLES DODDS. Cr. 8vo., price 5s.

THE LIFE MILITANT: Plain Sermons for Cottage Homes. By ELLELL. Crown 8vo., price 6s.

HOFER: A Drama. By CATHERINE SWANWICK. Demy 8vo., cloth, gilt edges, price 3s. 6d.

HISTORICAL SKETCHES OF THE REFORMATION. By the Rev. FREDERICK GEO. LEE, D.C.L., Vicar of All Saints', Lambeth, &c., &c., &c. One Volume, post octavo, 10s. 6d. cloth.

"The entire volume .... is well worth reading."—*Tablet.*
"Truly and graphically told."—*Academy.*

THE COMMERCIAL PRODUCTS OF THE SEA; or, Marine Contributions to Industry and Art. By P. L. SIMMONDS, Author of " The Commercial Products of the Vegetable Kingdom." One vol., with numerous Illustrations, 16s.

A GLOSSARY OF BIOLOGICAL, ANATOMICAL, AND PHYSIOLOGICAL TERMS, for Teachers and Students in Schools and Classes connected with the Science and Art Department, and other Examining bodies. By THOMAS DUNMAN, Physiology Lecturer at the Birkbeck Institution and the Working Men's College. Crown 8vo., cloth 2s. 6d.

THE CRIMEAN CAMPAIGN WITH THE CONNAUGHT RANGERS, 1854-55-56. By Lieut.-Colonel NATHANIEL STEEVENS, late 88th (Connaught Rangers). One volume, Demy 8vo., with Map, Scarlet Cloth, 15s.

" A welcome addition to the military history of England."—
United Service Gazette.

CHILD LIFE IN JAPAN, and Japanese
Child Stories. By M. CHAPLIN AYRTON (Bachelier-ès-Lettres, et Bachelier-ès-Sciences, Paris, Civis Academiæ Edinensis, and Elève de la Faculté de Médecine de Paris). With Seven full-page Illustrations, drawn and engraved by Japanese artists, and many smaller ones. Quarto, Cloth elegant, price 10s. 6d.

"People who give it away are likely to be tempted to buy a new copy to keep."—*Saturday Review.*

MEMORABLE BATTLES IN ENGLISH
HISTORY: The Military Lives of the Commanders. By W. H. DAVENPORT ADAMS. New and thoroughly Revised Edition. With Frontispiece and Plans of Battles. Two vols., Crown 8vo., Cloth. Price 16s.

"The materials for these two volumes have been carefully collected and the best authorities consulted, while the narrative is spirited, vigorous, and clear."—*Spectator.*

OCEAN AND HER RULERS: A Narrative
of the Nations which have from the Earliest Ages held Dominion over the Sea, comprising a Brief History of Navigation from the Remotest Periods up to the Present Time. By ALFRED ELWES. New, Enlarged, and thoroughly Revised Edition, with 16 Illustrations by WALTER W. MAY. Crown 8vo. Price 9s.

MASTERPIECES OF ANTIQUE ART.
From the celebrated collections in the Vatican, the Louvre, and the British Museum. By STEPHEN THOMPSON, Author of "Old English Homes," "Old Masters," &c. Twenty-five Examples in Permanent Photography. Super-Royal Quarto. Elegantly bound, price £2 2s.

WORKS BY JOHN TIMBS, F.S.A.

Notabilia, or CURIOUS AND AMUSING FACTS ABOUT MANY THINGS. Explained and Illustrated by JOHN TIMBS, F.S.A. Post 8vo, 6s.
"There is a world of wisdom in this book."—*Art Journal.*

Ancestral Stories and Traditions of Great Families. Illustrative of English History. With Frontispiece. Post 8vo, price 7s. 6d.
"An interesting and well written book."—*Literary Churchman.*

Strange Stories of the Animal World. A Book of Curious Contributions to Natural History. Illustrations by ZWECKER. Second Edition. Post 8vo, gilt edges, price 6s.
"Will be studied with profit and pleasure."—*Athenæum.*

Caxton's Fifteen O's and other Prayers. Printed by command of the Princess Elizabeth, Queen of England and France, and also of the Princess Margaret, mother of our Sovereign Lord the King. By WM. CAXTON. Reproduced in Photo-Lithography by S. Ayling. Quarto, bound in parchment. New and cheaper edition, price 6s.

The Day Dreams of a Sleepless Man: being a series of Papers contributed to the *Standard*, by FRANK IVES SCUDAMORE, Esq., C.B. Post 8vo, price 3s. 6d.
"Decidedly clever and full of good humour."—*Graphic*.

Mission from Cape Coast Castle to Ashantee. WITH A DESCRIPTIVE ACCOUNT OF THAT KINGDOM By the late T. EDWARD BOWDICH, ESQ. New Edition, with preface by his daughter, Mrs. HALE. With map of the route to Coomassie. Post 8vo. Price 5s.

Joan of Arc AND THE TIMES OF CHARLES THE SEVENTH. By Mrs. BRAY, Author of "Life of Stothard," etc. Post 8vo, price 7s. 6d.
"Readers will rise from its perusal, not only with increased information, but with sympathies awakened and elevated."—*Times*.

The Good St. Louis and His Times. By Mrs. BRAY. With Portrait. Post 8vo. price 7s. 6d.
"A valuable and interesting record of Louis' reign."—*Spectator*.

Sagas from the Far East, or KALMOUK AND MONGOLIAN TALES. With Historical Preface and Explanatory Notes by the Author of "Patrañas," etc. Post 8vo, price 9s.

Asem, the Man Hater: an Eastern Tale by OLIVER GOLDSMITH. With Illustrations and an Editorial Introduction. Price 2s.

The Vicar of Wakefield; a Tale by OLIVER GOLDSMITH. With eight Illustrations by JOHN ABSOLON. Beautifully printed by Whittingham. 3s. 6d. cloth; 10s. 6d. morocco antique.

STANESBY'S ILLUMINATED GIFT BOOKS.

Every page richly printed in Gold and Colours.

The Bridal Souvenir. New Edition, with a Portrait of the Princess Royal. Elegantly bound in white morocco, price 21s.
"A splendid specimen of decorative art, and well suited for a bridal gift."

The Birth-Day Souvenir. A Book of Thoughts on Life and Immortality. Price 12s. 6d. cloth; 18s. morocco antique.

Light for the Path of Life; from the Holy Scriptures. Small 4to, price 12s. cloth; 15s. calf, gilt edges; 18s. morocco antique.

The Wisdom of Solomon; from the Book of Proverbs. Small 4to, price 14s. cloth elegant; 18s. calf; 21s. morocco antique.

The Floral Gift. Price 14s. cloth elegant; 21s. morocco extra.

Shakespeare's Household Words. With a Photograph from the Monument at Stratford-on-Avon. New and Cheaper Edition, Price 6s. cloth elegant; 10s. 6d. morocco antique.

Aphorisms of the Wise and Good. With a Photographic Portrait of Milton. Price 6s. cloth elegant; 10s. 6d. Morocco antique.

POETRY.

Poems. By E. L. FLOYER. Fcap. 8vo, price 2s. 6d.

The Seasons; a Poem by the Rev. O. RAYMOND, LL.B. Fcap. 8vo, with Four Illustrations. Price 2s. 6d.

THREE BIRTHDAY BOOKS.

I. **The Book of Remembrance** for every Day in the Year. With blank space for recording Birthdays, Weddings, &c., &c. Beautifully printed in red and black. Imp. 32mo., prices from 2s. upwards. Or with photographs, from 5s.

* *May also be had in various leather Bindings.*

II. **The Churchman's Daily Remembrancer.** With Poetical Selections for the Christian Year, with Calendar and Table of Lessons of the English Church, for the use of both Clergy and Laity. Cloth elegant, price 2s.; or with Photographs, cloth elegant, 4s.

* *May also be had in various leather Bindings.*

III. **The Anniversary Text Book of Scripture Verse and Sacred Song** for Every Day in the Year. Cloth, 1s.; or, gilt edges, 1s. 6d.

* *May also be had in various leather Bindings.*

Emblems of Christian Life. Illustrated by W. HARRY ROGERS, in One Hundred Original Designs, from the Writings of the Fathers, Old English Poets, &c. Printed by Whittingham, with Borders and Initials in Red. Square 8vo. price 10s. 6d. cloth elegant, gilt edges; 21s. Turkey morocco antique.

Bishop Ken's Approach to the Holy Altar. With an Address to Young Communicants. Limp Cloth, 8d.; superior cloth, red edges, 1s.; with Photographs 2s. extra.

* *May also be had in various leather Bindings.*

* Clergymen wishing to introduce this Manual can have specimen copy, with prices for quantities, post free for six stamps, on application.

Confirmation; or Called, and Chosen, and Faithful. By the Author of "The Gospel in the Church's Seasons" series. With a Preface by The Very Reverend the DEAN OF CHESTER. Fcap. 8vo., Cloth, 1s.

A cheaper edition for distribution, price 9d.

An Illuminated Certificate of Confirmation and First Communion. Price 2d.

A New "In Memoriam" Card. Printed in silver or gold. Price 2d.

* *A reduction made on taking a quantity of the above cards.*

NEW BOOKS FOR CHILDREN
AND NEW EDITIONS OF OLD FAVOURITES.

THE FAVOURITE PICTURE BOOK, and Nursery Companion. Compiled anew by UNCLE CHARLIE. With four hundred and fifty Illustrations by ABSOLON, ANELAY, BENNETT, BROWNE (PHIZ), SIR JOHN GILBERT, T. LANDSEER, LEECH, PROUT, HARRISON WEIR, and others. Medium 4to, cloth elegant, price 5s.

Also published in the following four parts, price One Shilling each:—

| THE PICTURESQUE PRIMER. | EASY READING FOR LITTLE READERS. |
| FRAGMENTS OF KNOWLEDGE FOR LITTLE FOLK. | THE NURSERY COMPANION. |

Each in an attractive Paper Cover.

GOLDEN THREADS FROM AN ANCIENT LOOM; *Das Nibelungenlied* adapted to the use of Young Readers. By LYDIA HANDS. Dedicated by permission to THOMAS CARLYLE. With Fourteen Wood Engravings by J. SCHNORR, of Carolsfeld. Royal 4to. Price 10s. 6d.

THE BIRD AND INSECTS POST OFFICE. By ROBERT BLOOMFIELD, Author of "The Farmer's Boy." Illustrated with Thirty-five Wood Engravings. Crown 4to. 6s.

MODEL YACHTS and **Model Yacht Sailing.** How to Build, Rig, and Sail a self-acting model Yacht. By JAS. E. WALTON, V.M.Y.C. Fcap. 4to, with 52 Woodcuts.

THE ENGLISH STRUWWELPETER; or, Pretty Stories and Funny Pictures for Little Children. After the 110th Edition of the celebrated German Work, Dr. HEINRICH HOFFMANN. Twenty-sixth Edition. Twenty-four pages of Illustrations. Paper Boards, 4to. Price 2s. 6d.

LITTLE MARGARET'S RIDE TO THE ISLE OF WIGHT; or the Wonderful Rocking Horse. By Mrs. FREDERICK BROWN. With eight Illustrations in chromo-lithography by her sister, HELEN S. TATHAM. Crown 4to.

THE YOUNG VOCALIST. A collection of Twelve Songs, each with an Accompaniment for the Pianoforte. By Mrs. MOUNSEY BARTHOLOMEW. New and cheaper Edition. Paper, price 1s., cloth limp, price 2s.

KITTY AND BO: or the Story of a very little Girl and Boy. By A. T. Crown 8vo, illustrated.

NEW AND POPULAR WORKS

THE LITTLE PILGRIM. With Numerous Pen and Ink Sketches by HELEN PETRIE.

HAND SHADOWS to be thrown upon the Wall. Novel and amusing figures formed by the hand. By HENRY BURSILL. New and cheaper edition. Twelfth Thousand. Two series in one, price 1s. Crown 4to.

THE YOUNG BUGLERS: A Tale of the Peninsular War. By G. A. HENTY, Author of "Out on the Pampas," &c. With Eight full-page pictures by J. PROCTOR, and numerous plans of Battles. Large Crown 8vo, 7s. 6d.

WORKMAN AND SOLDIER. A Tale of Paris Life during the Siege and the rule of the Commune. By JAMES F. COBB, Author of "Silent Jim," "Watchers on the Long-ships," &c. With Illustrations and a Frontispiece by HARRY FURNISS. Crown 8vo, 5s.

THE MEN OF THE BACKWOODS: or, Stories and Sketches of the Indians and the Indian Fighters. By ASCOTT R. HOPE, author of "Heroes of Young America," &c., &c. Thirty-three Illustrations by C. O. MURRAY. Crown 8vo. Price 6s.

WILL WEATHERHELM: or, the Yarn of an Old Sailor about his Early Life and Adventures. By W. H. G. KINGSTON. Illustrated by W. W. MAY and G. H. THOMAS. New and Enlarged Edition. Imperial 16mo. Price 6s.; or bevelled boards, gilt edges, 7s. 6d.

CORNERTOWN CHRONICLES. New Legends of Old Lore written for the young. By KATHLEEN KNOX, author of "Queen Dora," &c. Crown 8vo., fully Illustrated by H. J. DAKIN. Price 4s. 6d., gilt edges, 5s.

SILVER LININGS: or, Light and Shade. By Mrs. REGINALD M. BRAY, author of "Ten of Them," &c. With Illustrations by A. H. COLLINS. Crown 8vo. 4s. 6d., gilt edges, 5s.

SILLY PETER; A Queer Story of a Daft Boy, a Prince, and a Miller's Daughter. By W. NORRIS. Illustrated. Crown 8vo. Price 2s. 6d.

BUNCHY: or, The Children of Scarsbrook Farm. By Miss E. C. PHILLIPS, author of "The Orphans," &c. Illustrations by A. J. JOHNSON. Crown 8vo. 2s. 6d.

PUBLISHED BY GRIFFITH AND FARRAN. 11

WAYS AND TRICKS OF ANIMALS, with Stories about Aunt Mary's Pets. By Miss MARY HOOPER, author of "Wives and Housewives," "Little Dinners," &c. With Twenty-three full-page Illustrations. Crown 8vo. 2s. 6d.

AFRICAN PETS: or, Chats about our Animal Friends in Natal, with a Sketch of Kaffir Life. By F. CLINTON PARRY. Illustrated by R. H. MOORE. Cr. 8vo. 2s. 6d.

A NEW ONE SHILLING SERIES.

WRECKED, NOT LOST: or, the Pilot and his Companion. By the Hon. Mrs. DUNDAS. Illustrated. New and cheaper edition. Fifth Thousand. Fcap. 8vo., price 1s.

AMONG THE BRIGANDS, and other Tales of Adventure. Illustrated. New and cheaper edition. Fourth Thousand. Fcap. 8vo., price 1s.

CHRISTIAN ELLIOTT: or, Mrs. Danvers' Prize. By L. N. COMYN. Illustrated. New and cheaper edition. Fourth Thousand. Fcap. 8vo., 1s.

FAVOURITE LIBRARY.
Monthly Volumes, including Mrs. HOFLAND's
"Son of a Genius,"   "Ellen the Teacher,"
"Daughter of a Genius,"   "Theodore; or, The Crusaders,"
&c. Medium 16mo., price 1s. each.
For complete List of Series, see page 26.

HAPPY HOLIDAYS: or, Brothers and Sisters at Home. By EMMA DAVENPORT. Illustrated. New and cheaper edition. Fourth Thousand. Fcap. 8vo., 1s. 6d.

ADVENTURES IN AUSTRALIA: or, the Wanderings of Captain Spencer in the Bush and the Wilds. By Mrs. R. LEE. New and revised edition. Illustrated. Sixth Thousand. 3s. 6d., gilt edges, 4s.

A WORD TO THE WISE: or, Hints on the Current Improprieties of Expression in Writing and Speaking. By PARRY GWYNNE. Sixteenth Thousand, revised. 18mo., price 6d., sewed; or 1s. cloth, gilt edges.

HARRY HAWKINS'S H-BOOK; showing how he learned to aspirate his H's. Eighth Thousand. 18mo. Uniform with "A Word to the Wise." Price 6d.

Six Shillings each, cloth elegant, with Illustrations.

***Kingston's** (W. H. G.) **Will Weatherhelm**: OR, THE YARN OF AN OLD SAILOR ABOUT HIS EARLY LIFE AND ADVENTURES.
* ,, **The Missing Ship,** OR NOTES FROM THE LOG OF THE "OUZEL GALLEY."
* ,, **The Three Admirals,** AND THE ADVENTURES OF THEIR YOUNG FOLLOWERS.
* ,, **The Three Lieutenants**; or, NAVAL LIFE IN THE NINETEENTH CENTURY.
* ,, **The Three Commanders**; OR, ACTIVE SERVICE AFLOAT IN MODERN TIMES.
* ,, **The Three Midshipmen.** New Edition, with 24 Illustrations by G. THOMAS, PORTCH, etc.
* ,, **Hurricane Hurry,** or THE ADVENTURES OF A NAVAL OFFICER DURING THE AMERICAN WAR OF INDEPENDENCE.
* ,, **True Blue; or, The Life and Adventures of a British** SEAMAN OF THE OLD SCHOOL.

The Men of the Backwoods: OR, STORIES AND SKETCHES OF THE INDIANS AND THE INDIAN FIGHTERS. By ASCOTT R. HOPE.

Ice Maiden AND OTHER STORIES. By HANS CHRISTIAN ANDERSEN. 89 Illustrations by ZWECKER. 4to., *Gilt edges.*

***Journey to the Centre of the Earth.** Authorized Translation. From the French of JULES VERNE. With 53 Illustrations.

The Bird and Insects Post Office. By ROBERT BLOOMFIELD. Illustrated with Thirty-five Illustrations. Crown 4to.

Little Maids. Rhymes with Illustrations by Mrs. W. KEMP. Quarto, gilt edges.

*The Books marked * may be had with bevelled boards, gilt edges, price 7s. 6d.*

Five Shillings each, cloth elegant; or Five Shillings and Sixpence, gilt edges. Illustrated by eminent Artists.

Chums: A Story for the Youngsters, of Schoolboy Life and Adventure. By HARLEIGH SEVERNE.

Early Start in Life (The). By EMILIA MARRYAT NORRIS.

Gentleman Cadet (The): HIS CAREER AND ADVENTURES AT THE ROYAL ACADEMY, WOOLWICH. By LIEUT.-COLONEL DRAYSON.

Gerald and Harry, or THE BOYS IN THE NORTH. By EMILIA MARRYAT NORRIS.

Five Shillings each—continued.

Hair-Breadth Escapes, or THE ADVENTURES OF THREE BOYS IN SOUTH AFRICA. By the Rev. H. C. ADAMS.
Heroes of the Crusades. By BARBARA HUTTON.
Home Life in the Highlands. By LILIAS GRAEME.
Household Stories from the land of Hofer, or POPULAR MYTHS OF TIROL, INCLUDING THE ROSE GARDEN OF KING LARYN.
Kingston's (W. H. G.) John Deane of Nottingham, HIS ADVENTURES AND EXPLOITS.
  ,,   Rival Crusoes (The). (*Or bevelled boards, gilt edges,* 6s.)
Out on the Pampas, or THE YOUNG SETTLERS. By G. A. HENTY.
Patrañas, or SPANISH STORIES, LEGENDARY AND TRADITIONAL. By the Author of "Household Stories."
Swift and Sure, or THE CAREER OF TWO BROTHERS. By A. ELWES.
Tales of the Saracens. By BARBARA HUTTON.
Tales of the White Cockade. By BARBARA HUTTON.
Wilton of Cuthbert's: A TALE OF UNDERGRADUATE LIFE THIRTY YEARS AGO. By the Rev. H. C. Adams.
Young Franc Tireurs (The), AND THEIR ADVENTURES DURING THE FRANCO-PRUSSIAN WAR. By G. A. HENTY, Special Correspondent of the *Standard*.

Five Shillings each, cloth, Illustrated, gilt edges.

Elwes' (A.) Luke Ashleigh, or SCHOOL LIFE IN HOLLAND.
  ,,   **Paul Blake,** or A BOY'S PERILS IN CORSICA AND MONTE CRISTO.
Neptune's Heroes, or THE SEA KINGS OF ENGLAND, FROM HAWKINS TO FRANKLIN. By W. H. DAVENPORT ADAMS.
Talks about Plants, or EARLY LESSONS IN BOTANY. By Mrs. LANKESTER. With six Coloured Plates and numerous Wood Engravings.

A NEW UNIFORM SERIES OF FIVE SHILLING VOLS.
Square Crown 8vo., gilt edges.

The Day of Wonders: A MEDLEY OF SENSE AND NONSENSE. By M. SULLIVAN. 30 Illustrations by W. G. BROWNE.
Harty the Wanderer; or, CONDUCT IS FATE. A Tale by FAIRLEIGH OWEN. 28 Illustrations by JOHN PROCTOR.
A Wayside Posy. GATHERED FOR GIRLS. By F. LABLACHE. 15 Illustrations by A. H. COLLINS.

Price Five Shillings each, cloth elegant, Illustrated.

Extraordinary Nursery Rhymes; New, yet Old. Translated from the Original Jingle into Comic Verse by One who was once a Child. 60 Illustrations. Small 4to.

Favourite Picture Book (The) and Nursery Companion. Compiled anew by UNCLE CHARLIE. With 450 Illustrations by ABSOLON, ANELAY, BENNETT, BROWNE (PHIZ), SIR JOHN GILBERT, T. LANDSEER, LEECH, PROUT, HARRISON WEIR, and others. Medium 4to., cloth elegant.

** This may also be had in Four Parts, in fancy wrapper, price 1s. each.

Little Gipsy (The). By ELIE SAUVAGE. Translated by ANNA BLACKWELL. Profusely illustrated by ERNEST FRÖLICH. Small 4to,; (or, extra cloth, *gilt edges*, 6s.)

Norstone; or, RIFTS IN THE CLOUDS. By M. E. HATTERSLEY.

Merry Songs for Little Voices. Words by Mrs. BRODERIP. Music by THOMAS MURBY. With 40 Illustrations. Fcap. 4to.

Stories from the Old and New Testaments. By the Rev. B. H. DRAPER. With 48 Engravings.

Trimmer's History of the Robins. Written for the Instruction of Children on their treatment of Animals. With 24 Illustrations by HARRISON WEIR. Small 4to, gilt edges.

Workman and Soldier. A TALE OF PARIS LIFE DURING THE SIEGE AND THE RULE OF THE COMMUNE. By JAMES F. COBB.

Four Shillings and Sixpence each, cloth elegant, with Illustrations; or with gilt edges, 5s.

Alda Graham; and her Brother Philip. By E. MARRYAT NORRIS.

Book of Cats (The): a Chit-chat Chronicle of Feline Facts and Fancies. By CHARLES H. ROSS.

"Buttons." THE TRIALS AND TRAVELS OF A YOUNG GENTLEMAN. By ASCOTT R. HOPE.

Casimir, the Little Exile. By CAROLINE PEACHEY.

Cornertown Chronicles. NEW LEGENDS OF OLD LORE WRITTEN FOR THE YOUNG. By KATHLEEN KNOX.

Favourite Fables in Prose and Verse. With 24 beautiful Illustrations from Drawings by HARRISON WEIR. Small 4to.

Fiery Cross (The), OR THE VOW OF MONTROSE. By BARBARA HUTTON.

PUBLISHED BY GRIFFITH AND FARRAN. 15

Four Shillings and Sixpence each—continued.

Mandarin's Daughter (The): A STORY OF THE GREAT TAEPING REBELLION. By SAMUEL MOSSMAN.

Modern British Plutarch (The), or LIVES OF MEN DISTINGUISHED IN THE RECENT HISTORY OF OUR COUNTRY FOR THEIR TALENTS, VIRTUES, AND ACHIEVEMENTS. By W. C. TAYLOR, LL.D.

Oak Staircase, (The) or THE STORIES OF LORD AND LADY DESMOND a Narrative of the Times of James II. By M. and C. LEE.

Silver Linings: or, LIGHT AND SHADE. By Mrs. REGINALD M. BRAY.

Tales and Legends of Saxony and Lusatia. By W. WESTALL.

Theodora: a Tale for Girls. By EMILIA MARRYAT NORRIS.

Zipporah, the Jewish Maiden. By M. E. BEWSHER.

Three Shillings and Sixpence plain ; or coloured plates and gilt edges, Four Shillings and Sixpence, Super Royal 16mo, cloth elegant, with Illustrations.

Aunt Jenny's American Pets. By CATHERINE C. HOPLEY.

Broderip (Mrs.) Crosspatch, the Cricket, and the Counterpane.
,, My Grandmother's Budget OF STORIES AND VERSES.
,, Tales of the Toys. TOLD BY THEMSELVES.
,, Tiny Tadpole, AND OTHER TALES.

Cousin Trix, AND HER WELCOME TALES. By GEORGIANA CRAIK.

Cosmorama: THE MANNERS AND CUSTOMS OF ALL NATIONS OF THE WORLD DESCRIBED. By J. ASPIN.

Distant Homes, or THE GRAHAM FAMILY IN NEW ZEALAND. By Mrs. I. E. AYLMER.

Early Days of English Princes. By Mrs. RUSSELL GRAY.

Echoes of an Old Bell. By the Hon. AUGUSTA BETHELL.

Facts to Correct Fancies, or SHORT NARRATIVES OF REMARKABLE WOMEN.

Fairy Land, or RECREATION FOR THE RISING GENERATION, in Prose and Verse. By THOMAS and JANE HOOD. Illustrated by T. HOOD, Jun.

Feathers and Fairies, or STORIES FROM THE REALMS OF FANCY. By the Hon. AUGUSTA BETHELL.

Garden (The), or FREDERICK'S MONTHLY INSTRUCTION FOR THE MANAGEMENT AND FORMATION OF A FLOWER GARDEN. With Illustrations by SOWERBY. *6s. coloured.*

NEW AND POPULAR WORKS

Three Shillings and Sixpence each—continued.

Hacco the Dwarf, or THE TOWER ON THE MOUNTAIN, and other Tales. By LADY LUSHINGTON.

Happy Home (The), or THE CHILDREN AT THE RED HOUSE. By LADY LUSHINGTON.

Helen in Switzerland. By the Hon. AUGUSTA BETHELL.

Holidays among the Mountains, or SCENES AND STORIES OF WALES. By M. BETHAM EDWARDS.

Lightsome and the Little Golden Lady. Written and Illustrated by C. H. BENNETT Twenty-four Engravings.

Nursery Times, or STORIES ABOUT THE LITTLE ONES. By an Old Nurse.

Play Room Stories, or HOW TO MAKE PEACE. By GEORGIANA M. CRAIK.

Peep at the Pixies (A), or LEGENDS OF THE WEST. By Mrs. BRAY.

Scenes and Stories of the Rhine. By M. BETHAM EDWARDS.

Seven Birthdays (The), or THE CHILDREN OF FORTUNE. By KATHLEEN KNOX.

Starlight Stories, TOLD TO BRIGHT EYES AND LISTENING EARS. By FANNY LABLACHE.

Stories of Edward, AND HIS LITTLE FRIENDS.

Tales of Magic and Meaning. Written and Illustrated by ALFRED CROWQUILL.

Visits to Beechwood Farm. By CATHARINE COWPER.

Three Shillings and Sixpence plain, cloth elegant, with Illustrations by eminent Artists, or with gilt edges, price 4s.

Almeria's Castle, or MY EARLY LIFE IN INDIA AND ENGLAND. By LADY LUSHINGTON.

Cast Adrift, the Story of a Waif. By Mrs. HERBERT MARTIN.

Castles and their Heroes. By BARBARA HUTTON.

Clement's Trial and Victory, or SOWING AND REAPING. By M. E. B. (Mrs. GELLIE). Third Thousand.

Faggots for the Fireside, or TALES OF FACT AND FANCY. By PETER PARLEY.

PUBLISHED BY GRIFFITH AND FARRAN. 17

Three Shillings and Sixpence each—continued.

Great and Small; SCENES IN THE LIFE OF CHILDREN. Translated, with permission, from the French of Mdlle. Laroque, by Miss HARRIET POOLE. With 61 Illustrations by BERTALL.

Grey Towers; or AUNT HETTY'S WILL. By M. M. POLLARD.

Isabel's Difficulties, or LIGHT ON THE DAILY PATH. By M. R. CAREY.

Joachim's Spectacles: A LEGEND OF FLORENTIAL. By M. & C. LEE.

Kingston's (W.H.G.) Fred Markham in Russia, or, THE BOY TRAVELLERS IN THE LAND OF THE CZAR.

,, Manco the Peruvian Chief.
,, Mark Seaworth; a Tale of the Indian Ocean.
,, Peter the Whaler; HIS EARLY LIFE AND ADVENTURES IN THE ARCTIC REGIONS.
,, Salt Water, or NEIL D'ARCY'S SEA LIFE AND ADVENTURES.

Lee (Mrs.) Anecdotes of the Habits and Instincts of Animals.
,, Anecdotes of the Habits and Instincts of Birds, Reptiles, and Fishes.
,, Adventures in Australia, or THE WANDERINGS OF CAPTAIN SPENCER IN THE BUSH AND THE WILDS.
,, The African Wanderers, or CARLOS AND ANTONIO.

Little May's Friends, or COUNTRY PETS AND PASTIMES. By ANNIE WHITTEM.

Louisa Broadhurst; or FIRST EXPERIENCES. By A. M.

My School Days in Paris. By MARGARET S. JEUNE.

Meadow Lea, or THE GIPSY CHILDREN.

Millicent and Her Cousins. By the Hon. AUGUSTA BETHELL.

New Girl (The), or THE RIVALS; a Tale of School Life. By M. E. B. (Mrs. GELLIE).

North Pole (The); AND HOW CHARLIE WILSON DISCOVERED IT. By the Author of "Realms of the Ice King," &c.

Our Old Uncle's Home; AND WHAT THE BOYS DID THERE. By Mother CAREY.

Queen Dora: THE LIFE AND LESSONS OF A LITTLE GIRL. By KATHLEEN KNOX.

Rosamond Fane, or THE PRISONERS OF ST. JAMES. By M. and C. LEE.

Talent in Tatters, or SOME VICISSITUDES IN THE LIFE OF AN ENGLISH BOY. By HOPE WRAYTHE.

Three Shillings and Sixpence each—continued.

The **Triumphs of Steam,** or STORIES FROM THE LIVES OF WATT, ARKWRIGHT, AND STEPHENSON.

The **Whispers of a Shell,** or STORIES OF THE SEA. By FRANCES FREELING BRODERIP.

Wild Roses, or SIMPLE STORIES OF COUNTRY LIFE. By the same.

Three Shillings and Sixpence each, cloth elegant, Illustrated.

Among the Zulus. By LIEUT-COL. DRAYSON. Cloth, gilt edges.

Attractive Picture Book (The). A New Gift Book from the Old Corner, containing numerous Illustrations by eminent Artists. *Bound in Elegant Paper Boards, Royal 4to, price 3s. 6d. each plain; 7s. 6d. coloured; 10s. 6d. mounted on cloth and coloured.*

Berries and Blossoms: a Verse Book for Young People. By T. WESTWOOD.

Bible Illustrations, or A DESCRIPTION OF MANNERS AND CUSTOMS PECULIAR TO THE EAST. By the Rev. B. H. DRAPER. Revised by Dr. KITTO.

British History Briefly Told (The), AND A DESCRIPTION OF THE ANCIENT CUSTOMS, SPORTS, AND PASTIMES OF THE ENGLISH.

Clara Hope, or THE BLADE AND THE EAR. By Miss MILNER. Frontispiece by BIRKET FOSTER.

Four Seasons (The); A Short Account of the Structure of Plants being Four Lectures written for the Working Men's Institute, Paris. With Illustrations. Imperial 16mo.

Family Bible Newly Opened (The); WITH UNCLE GOODWIN'S ACCOUNT OF IT. By JEFFREYS TAYLOR. Fcap. 8vo.

Glimpses of Nature, AND OBJECTS OF INTEREST DESCRIBED DURING A VISIT TO THE ISLE OF WIGHT. By Mrs. LOUDON. Forty-one Illustrations.

History of the Robins (The). By Mrs. TRIMMER. In Words of One Syllable. Edited by the Rev. CHARLES SWETE, M.A.

Historical Acting Charades, or AMUSEMENTS FOR WINTER EVENINGS. By the Author of "Cat and Dog," etc. Fcap. 8vo.

How to be Happy, or FAIRY GIFTS.

Infant Amusements, or HOW TO MAKE A NURSERY HAPPY. With Practical Hints on the Moral and Physical Training of Children. By W. H. G. KINGSTON.

PUBLISHED BY GRIFFITH AND FARRAN. 19

Three Shillings and Sixpence each—continued.

Man's Boot (The), AND OTHER STORIES IN WORDS OF ONE SYLLABLE. Illustrations by HARRISON WEIR. 4to., gilt edges.

The Mine, or SUBTERRANEAN WONDERS. An Account of the Operations of the Miner and the Products of his Labours.

Modern Sphinx (The). A Collection of ENIGMAS, CHARADES, REBUSES, DOUBLE AND TRIPLE ACROSTICS, ANAGRAMS, LOGOGRIPHS, METAGRAMS, VERBAL PUZZLES, CONUNDRUMS, etc. Fcap. 8vo, price 3s. 6d.; gilt edges, 4s.

Root and Flower. By JOHN PALMER.

Sunbeam: a Fairy Tale. By Mrs. PIETZKER.

Sylvia's New Home, a Story for the Young. By Mrs. J. F. B. FIRTH.

Taking Tales for Cottage Homes. In Plain Language and Large Type. Two vols.

May also be had in 4 vols, 1s. 6d. each; and 12 parts, 4d. each.

Three Shillings and Sixpence plain; Five Shillings coloured.

Bear King (The): a Narrative confided to the Marines by JAMES GREENWOOD. With Illustrations by ERNEST GRISET. Small 4to.

Familiar Natural History. With 42 Illustrations by HARRISON WEIR.

*** Also, in Two Vols., entitled "British Animals and Birds," "Foreign Animals and Birds." 2s. each, plain; 2s. 6d. coloured.

Old Nurse's Book of Rhymes, Jingles, and Ditties. Illustrated by C. H. BENNETT. Ninety Engravings.

Three Shillings, or gilt edges, Three and Sixpence.

Our Soldiers, or ANECDOTES OF THE CAMPAIGNS AND GALLANT DEEDS OF THE BRITISH ARMY DURING THE REIGN OF HER MAJESTY QUEEN VICTORIA. By W H. G. KINGSTON. With Frontispiece. New and Revised Edition. Eighth Thousand.

Our Sailors, or ANECDOTES OF THE ENGAGEMENTS AND GALLANT DEEDS OF THE BRITISH NAVY. With Frontispiece. New and Revised Edition. Eighth Thousand.

Lucy's Campaign: a Story of Adventure. By M. and C. LEE. Gilt edges.

Fruits of Enterprise, EXHIBITED IN THE TRAVELS OF BELZONI IN EGYPT AND NUBIA. With Six Engravings by BIRKET FOSTER.

Two Shillings and Sixpence plain, Super Royal 16mo, cloth elegant, with Illustrations by Harrison Weir and others.

Adventures and Experiences of Biddy Dorking and of the Fat Frog. Edited by Mrs. S. C. HALL.
Alice and Beatrice. By GRANDMAMMA.
Amy's Wish, and What Came of It. By Mrs. TYLEE.
Animals and their Social Powers. By MARY TURNER-ANDREWES.
Cat and Dog, or MEMOIRS OF PUSS AND THE CAPTAIN.
Crib and Fly: a Tale of Two Terriers.
Discontented Children (The), AND HOW THEY WERE CURED. By M. and E. KIRBY.
Doll and Her Friends (The), or MEMOIRS OF THE LADY SERAPHINA. By the Author of "Cat and Dog."
Early Dawn (The), or STORIES TO THINK ABOUT.
Every Inch a King, or THE STORY OF REX AND HIS FRIENDS. By Mrs. J. WORTHINGTON BLISS.
Fairy Gifts, or A WALLET OF WONDERS. By KATHLEEN KNOX.
Faithful Hound (The): (GELERT) a Story in Verse, founded on Fact. By LADY THOMAS.
Funny Fables for Little Folks.
Fun and Earnest, or RHYMES WITH REASON. By D'ARCY W. THOMPSON. Illustrated by C. H. BENNETT. Imperial 16mo.
Gerty and May. Eighth Thousand.

By the same Author.

Granny's Story Box. New Edition. With 20 Engravings.
Children of the Parsonage. | Sunny Days, OR A MONTH AT
Our White Violet. | THE GREAT STOWE.
The New Baby.

Jack Frost and Betty Snow; with other Tales for Wintry Nights and Rainy Days.
Julia Maitland, or, PRIDE GOES BEFORE A FALL. BY M. & E. KIRBY.
Lost in the Jungle; A TALE OF THE INDIAN MUTINY. By AUGUSTA MARRYAT.
Madelon. By ESTHER CARR.
Neptune: or THE AUTOBIOGRAPHY OF A NEWFOUNDLAND DOG.

Two Shillings and Sixpence each—continued.
Norris (Emilia Marryat.) A Week by Themselves.
By the same Author.

Adrift on the Sea.
Children's Pic-Nic (The).
Geoffry's Great Fault.
Harry at School.
Paul Howard's Captivity.

Seaside Home.
Snowed Up.
Stolen Cherries.
What became of Tommy.

Odd Stories about Animals: told in Short and Easy Words.
Our Home in the Marsh Land, or DAYS OF AULD LANG SYNE. By E. L. F.
Scripture Histories for Little Children. With Sixteen Illustrations by JOHN GILBERT
  CONTENTS :—The History of Joseph—History of Moses—History of our Saviour—The Miracles of Christ.
  Sold separately 6d. each, plain; 1s. coloured.
Secret of Wrexford (The), or STELLA DESMOND'S SECRET. By ESTHER CARR.
Story of Jack and the Giants. 35 Illustrations by RICHARD DOYLE.
Stories of Julian and His Playfellows. Written by his MAMMA.
Tales from Catland. Dedicated to the Young Kittens of England. By an OLD TABBY. Seventh Thousand.
Talking Bird (The), or THE LITTLE GIRL WHO KNEW WHAT WAS GOING TO HAPPEN. By M. and E. KIRBY.
Ten of Them, or THE CHILDREN OF DANEHURST. By Mrs. R. M. BRAY.
"Those Unlucky-Twins!" By A. LYSTER.
Tiny Stories for Tiny Readers in Tiny Words.
Tittle Tattle; and other Stories for Children. By the Author of "Little Tales for Tiny Tots," etc.
Trottie's Story Book: True Tales in Short Words and Large Type.
Tuppy, or THE AUTOBIOGRAPHY OF A DONKEY.
Wandering Blindfold, or A BOY'S TROUBLES. By MARY ALBERT.

Two Shillings and Sixpence, with Illustrations, cloth elegant, or with gilt edges, Three Shillings.

A Child's Influence, or KATHLEEN AND HER GREAT UNCLE. By LISA LOCKYER.
Adventures of Kwei, the Chinese Girl. By M.E.B. (Mrs. GELLIE).

Two Shillings and Sixpence each—continued.

Bertrand Du Guesclin, the Hero of Brittany. By EMILE DE BONNECHOSE. Translated by MARGARET S. JEUNE.

Corner Cottage, and Its Inmates, or TRUST IN GOD. By FRANCES OSBORNE.

Davenport's (Mrs.) Constance and Nellie, or THE LOST WILL.

„ **Our Birthdays,** AND HOW TO IMPROVE THEM.

„ **The Holidays Abroad,** or RIGHT AT LAST.

Father Time's Story Book for the Little Ones. By KATHLEEN KNOX.

From Peasant to Prince, or THE LIFE OF ALEXANDER PRINCE MENSCHIKOFF. From the Russian by Madame PIETZKER.

William Allair, or RUNNING AWAY TO SEA. By Mrs. H. WOOD.

Two Shillings and Sixpence each, Illustrated.

Among the Zulus: the Adventures of Hans Sterk, South African Hunter and Pioneer. By LIEUT.-COLONEL A. W. DRAYSON, R.A.

Boy's Own Toy Maker (The): a Practical Illustrated Guide to the useful employment of Leisure Hours. By E. LANDELLS. 200 Illustrations.

Children of the Olden Time. By the Author of "A Trap to Catch a Sunbeam." 27 Illustrations. Imperial 16mo.

Fairy Tales. Published by command of her Bright Dazzlingness Gloriana, Queen of Fairyland. By a Soldier of the Queen.

Girl's Own Toy Maker (The), AND BOOK OF RECREATION. By E. and A. LANDELLS. With 200 Illustrations.

Little Child's Fable Book. Arranged Progressively in One, Two and Three Syllables. 16 Page Illus. (*4s. 6d. coloured, gilt edges.*)

Silly Peter: A QUEER STORY OF A DAFT BOY, A PRINCE, AND A MILLER'S DAUGHTER. By W. NORRIS.

Spring Time; or, Words in Season. A Book for Girls. By SIDNEY COX. Third Edition.

A NEW UNIFORM SERIES OF HALF-CROWN BOOKS.
Cloth elegant, fully Illustrated.

African Pets: or, CHATS ABOUT OUR ANIMAL FRIENDS IN NATAL, WITH A SKETCH OF KAFFIR LIFE. By F. CLINTON PARRY.

Bunchy: or, THE CHILDREN OF SCARSBROOK FARM. By Miss E. C. PHILLIPS, Author of "The Orphans," &c.

Ways and Tricks of Animals, WITH STORIES ABOUT AUNT MARY'S PETS. By Miss MARY HOOPER.

COMICAL PICTURE BOOKS.

Two Shillings and Sixpence each, Coloured Plates, fancy boards.

English Struwwelpeter (The): or PRETTY STORIES AND FUNNY PICTURES FOR LITTLE CHILDREN. After the 110th Edition of the celebrated German Work, Dr. HEINRICH HOFFMANN, Twenty-sixth Edition. Twenty-four pages of Illustrations.

Loves of Tom Tucker and Little Bo-Peep. Written and Illustrated by THOMAS HOOD.

Spectropia, or SURPRISING SPECTRAL ILLUSIONS, showing Ghosts everywhere, and of any Colour. By J. H. BROWN.

Upside Down: a Series of Amusing Pictures from Sketches by the late W. McCONNELL, with Verses by THOMAS HOOD.

Two Shillings, cloth elegant, with Illustrations, or with coloured plates, gilt edges, Three Shillings.

Fanny and Her Mamma, or EASY LESSONS FOR CHILDREN.

Good in Everything, or THE EARLY HISTORY OF GILBERT HARLAND. By Mrs. BARWELL.

Infantine Knowledge: a Spelling and Reading Book on a Popular Plan.

Little Lessons for Little Learners, in Words of One Syllable. By Mrs. BARWELL.

Mamma's Bible Stories, FOR HER LITTLE BOYS AND GIRLS.

Mamma's Bible Stories (A Sequel to).

Mamma's Lessons, FOR HER LITTLE BOYS AND GIRLS.

Silver Swan (The): a Fairy Tale. By MADAME DE CHATELAIN.

Tales of School Life. By AGNES LOUDON.

Wonders of Home, in Eleven Stories (The). By GRANDFATHER GREY.

Two Shillings each.

Confessions of a Lost Dog (The). Reported by her Mistress, FRANCES POWER COBBE. With a Photograph of the Dog from Life, by FRANK HAES.

Home Amusements: a Choice Collection of Riddles, Charades, Conundrums, Parlour Games, and Forfeits.

How to Make Dolls' Furniture AND TO FURNISH A DOLL'S HOUSE. With 70 Illustrations. Small 4to.

Two Shillings each—continued.

Illustrated Paper Model Maker. By E. LANDELLS.
Rhymes and Pictures ABOUT BREAD, TEA, SUGAR, COTTON, COALS, AND GOLD. By WILLIAM NEWMAN. Seventy-two Illustrations. Price 2s. *plain;* 3s. 6d. *coloured.*
*** Each Subject may be had separately. 6d. *plain;* 1s. *coloured.*
Scenes of Animal Life and Character, FROM NATURE AND RECOLLECTION. In Twenty Plates. By J. B. 4to, fancy boards.
Sunday Evenings with Sophia, or LITTLE TALKS ON GREAT SUBJECTS. By L. G. BELL.
Surprising Adventures of the Clumsy Boy Crusoe (The). By CHARLES H. ROSS. With Twenty-three Coloured Illustrations.

A NEW UNIFORM SERIES.

Price One Shilling and Sixpence each, cloth elegant, fully Illustrated.

Angelo; or, THE PINE FOREST IN THE ALPS. By GERALDINE E. JEWSBURY. 5th Thousand.
Aunt Annette's Stories to Ada. By ANNETTE A. SALAMAN.
Brave Nelly; or, WEAK HANDS AND A WILLING HEART. By M.E.B (Mrs. GELLIE). Fifth Thousand.
Featherland; or, HOW THE BIRDS LIVED AT GREENLAWN. By G. M. FENN. 4th Thousand.
Humble Life: a Tale of HUMBLE HOMES. By the Author of "Gerty and May," &c.
Kingston's (W. H. G.) Child of the Wreck: or, THE LOSS OF THE ROYAL GEORGE.
Lee's (Mrs. R.) Playing at Settlers; or, THE FAGGOT HOUSE.
———————— Twelve Stories of the Sayings and Doings of Animals.
Little Lisette, THE ORPHAN OF ALSACE. By M.E.B. (Mrs. GELLIE).
Live Toys; OR, ANECDOTES OF OUR FOUR-LEGGED AND OTHER PETS. By EMMA DAVENPORT.
Long Evenings; or, STORIES FOR MY LITTLE FRIENDS. By EMILIA MARRYATT.
Three Wishes (The). By M.E.B. (Mrs. GELLIE).

PUBLISHED BY GRIFFITH AND FARRAN. 25

Price One Shilling and Sixpence each, cloth elegant, Illustrated.

Always Happy, or, ANECDOTES OF FELIX AND HIS SISTER SERENA. By a Mother. Twentieth Thousand.

Every-Day Things, or USEFUL KNOWLEDGE RESPECTING THE PRINCIPAL ANIMAL, VEGETABLE, AND MINERAL SUBSTANCES IN COMMON USE.

Grandmamma's Relics, AND HER STORIES ABOUT THEM. By E. E. BOWEN.

Happy Holidays: or, BROTHERS AND SISTERS AT HOME. By EMMA DAVENPORT. New and cheaper Edition.

Holiday Tales. By FLORENCE WILFORD. Author of "Nigel Bartram's Ideal," etc.

Kingston (W. H. G.) The Heroic Wife; or, THE ADVENTURES OF A FAMILY ON THE BANKS OF THE AMAZON.

Little Roebuck (The), from the German. Illustrated by LOSSON. Fancy boards (2s. coloured).

Taking Tales for Cottage Homes. In Plain Language and Large Type. Four vols.

May also be had in Two vols., 3s. 6d. each; or in the following 12 parts, price 4d. each.

N.B.—Each Tale is complete in itself.

1. The Miller of Hillbrook: A RURAL TALE.
2. Tom Trueman, A SAILOR IN A MERCHANTMAN.
3. Michael Hale and his Family in Canada.
4. John Armstrong, THE SOLDIER.
5. Joseph Rudge, THE AUSTRALIAN SHEPHERD.
6. Life Underground; OR DICK, THE COLLIERY BOY.
7. Life on the Coast; OR THE LITTLE FISHER GIRL.
8. Adventures of Two Orphans in London.
9. Early Days on Board a Man-of-War.
10. Walter, the Foundling: A TALE OF OLDEN TIMES.
11. The Tenants of Sunnyside Farm.
12. Holmwood: OR, THE NEW ZEALAND SETTLER.

Trimmer's (Mrs.) New Testament Lessons. With 40 Engravings.

A NEW UNIFORM SERIES OF SHILLING VOLUMES.
Cloth elegant, Illustrated.

Among the Brigands, and other Tales of Adventure. New and cheaper Edition. Fourth Thousand.

Christian Elliott: or, MRS. DANVER'S PRIZE. By L. N. COMYN. New and cheaper Edition. Fourth Thousand.

Wrecked, Not Lost; or THE PILOT AND HIS COMPANION. By the Hon. Mrs. DUNDAS. New and cheaper Edition. Fifth Thousand.

THE FAVOURITE LIBRARY.

New Editions of the Volumes in this Series are being issued, and other Volumes by Popular Authors will be added.

Cloth elegant, with coloured frontispiece and title-page, One Shilling each.

1. The Eskdale Herd Boy. By LADY STODDART.
2. Mrs. Leicester's School. By CHARLES and MARY LAMB.
3. The History of The Robins. By MRS. TRIMMER.
4. Memoir of Bob, The Spotted Terrier.
5. Keeper's Travels in Search of His Master.
6. The Scottish Orphans. By LADY STODDART.
7. Never Wrong; or, the Young Disputant; & It was only in Fun.
8. The Life and Perambulations of a Mouse.
9. The Son of a Genius. By MRS. HOFLAND.
10. The Daughter of a Genius. By MRS. HOFLAND.
11. Ellen, the Teacher. By MRS. HOFLAND.
12. Theodore; or, The Crusaders. By MRS. HOFLAND.
13. Right and Wrong. By the Author of "ALWAYS HAPPY."
14. Harry's Holiday. By JEFFERYS TAYLOR.
15. Short Poems and Hymns for Children.

Price One Shilling each, in various styles of binding.

The Picturesque Primer.
Fragments of Knowledge for Little Folk.
Easy Reading for Little Readers.
The Nursery Companion.

These Four Volumes contain about 450 pictures. Each one being complete in itself, and bound in an attractive paper cover.

The Four Volumes bound together form the "Favourite Picture Book," bound in cloth, price 5s.

Australian Babes in the Wood (The): a True Story told in Rhyme for the Young. Price 1s. boards, 1s. 6d. cloth, gilt edges.

Cowslip (The). Fully Illustrated cloth, 1s. *plain*; 1s. 6d. *coloured*.

Daisy (The). Fully Illustrated cloth, 1s *plain*; 1s. 6d. *coloured*.

Dame Partlett's Farm. AN ACCOUNT OF THE RICHES SHE OBTAINED BY INDUSTRY, &C. Coloured Illustrations, sewed.

One Shilling each—continued.

Female Christian Names, AND THEIR TEACHINGS. A Gift Book for Girls. By MARY E. BROMFIELD. Cloth, gilt edges.

Golden Words for Children, FROM THE BOOK OF LIFE. In English, French, and German. A set of Illuminated Cards in Packet. Or bound in cloth interleaved, price 2s. 6d. gilt edges.

Goody Two Shoes: or THE HISTORY OF LITTLE MARGERY MEANWELL IN RHYME. Fully Illustrated, cloth.

Hand Shadows, to be thrown upon the Wall. Novel and amusing figures formed by the hand. By HENRY BURSILL New and cheaper Edition. Twelfth Thousand. Two Series in one.

Headlong Career (The) and Woeful Ending of Precocious Piggy. By THOMAS HOOD. Illustrated by his Son. Printed in colours. Fancy wrapper, 4to. Or mounted on cloth, untearable, 2s.

Infant's Friend (The); or, EASY READING LESSONS FOR YOUNG CHILDREN. Coloured Illustrations, sewed.

Johnny Miller; OR TRUTH AND PERSEVERANCE. By FELIX WEISS.

Nine Lives of a Cat (The): a Tale of Wonder. Written and Illustrated by C. H. BENNETT. 24 Coloured Engravings, sewed.

Peter Piper PRACTICAL PRINCIPLES OF PLAIN AND PERFECT PRONUNCIATION. Coloured Illustrations, sewed.

Plaiting Pictures. A NOVEL PASTIME BY WHICH CHILDREN CAN CONSTRUCT AND RECONSTRUCT PICTURES FOR THEMSELVES. Four Series in Fancy Coloured Wrappers. Oblong 4to.
First Series.—Juvenile Party—Zoological Gardens—The Gleaner.
Second Series.—Birds' Pic-nic—Cats' Concert—Three Bears.
Third Series.—Blind Man's Buff—Children in the Wood—Snow Man.
Fourth Series.—Grandfather's Birthday—Gymnasium—Playroom.

Primrose Pilgrimage (The): a Woodland Story. By M. BETHAM EDWARDS. Illustrated by MACQUOID. Sewed.

Short and Simple Prayers, with Hymns for the Use of Children. By the Author of "Mamma's Bible Stories." Sixteenth Thousand. Cloth.

Whittington and his Cat. Coloured Illustrations, sewed.

DURABLE NURSERY BOOKS.

Mounted on cloth with coloured plates, One Shilling each.

1. COCK ROBIN.
2. COURTSHIP OF JENNY WREN.
3. DAME TROT AND HER CAT.
4. HOUSE THAT JACK BUILT.
5. PUSS IN BOOTS

Price Sixpence each, Plain ; One Shilling, coloured.

1. British Animals. 1st Series.
2. British Animals. 2nd Series.
3. British Birds.
4. Foreign Animals. 1st Series.
5. Foreign Animals. 2nd Series.
6. Foreign Birds.
7. The Farm and its Scenes.

} Illustrated by HARRISON WEIR.

8. The diverting history of John Gilpin.
9. The Peacock at home, and Butterfly's Ball.
10. History of Joseph.
11. History of Moses.
12. Life of our Saviour.
13. Miracles of Christ.

} Illustrated by JOHN GILBERT.

His name was Hero. By the Author of "The Four Seasons." Frontispiece by SIR W. CALCOTT, R.A. Super Royal 16mo. price 1s. sewed.

By the Same Author.

How I became a Governess. 3rd Edit. 2s. cloth; 2s. 6d., gilt edges.
My Pretty Puss. With Frontispiece. Price 6d.
The Grateful Sparrow: a True Story. Fifth Edition, price 6d.
The Adventures of a Butterfly. From the French of P. J. STAHL. Seven Engravings. Price 8d.
The Hare that Found his Way Home. From the French of P. J. STAHL. Second Edition. Price 6d.

WORKS FOR DISTRIBUTION.

A Woman's Secret; or, HOW TO MAKE HOME HAPPY. Thirty-third Thousand. 18mo, price 6d.

By the same Author, uniform in size and price.

Woman's Work; or, HOW SHE CAN HELP THE SICK. 19th Thousand.
A Chapter of Accidents; or, THE MOTHER'S ASSISTANT IN CASES OF BURNS, SCALDS, CUTS, &c. Ninth Thousand.
Pay to-day, Trust to-morrow; illustrating the Evils of the Tally System. Seventh Thousand.
Nursery Work; or, HANNAH BAKER'S FIRST PLACE. Fifth Thousand.
The Cook and the Doctor; or, CHEAP RECIPES AND USEFUL REMEDIES. Selected from the three first books. Price 2d.
Home Difficulties. A Few Words on the Servant Question. 4d.
Family Prayers for Cottage Homes. Price 2d.

PUBLISHED BY GRIFFITH AND FARRAN. 29

Educational Works.

HISTORY.

Britannia: a Collection of the Principal Passages in Latin Authors that refer to this Island, with Vocabulary and Notes. By T. S. CAYZER. Illustrated with a Map and 29 Woodcuts. Crown 8vo. Price 3s. 6d.

True Stories from Ancient History, chronologically arranged from the Creation of the World to the Death of Charlemagne. 12mo, 5s. cloth.

Mrs. Trimmer's Concise History of England, revised and brought down to the present Time. By Mrs. MILNER. With Portraits of the Sovereigns. 5s. cloth.

Rhymes of Royalty: the History of England in Verse, from the Norman Conquest to the reign of VICTORIA; with a summary of the leading events in each reign. Fcap. 8vo. 2s. cloth.

GEOGRAPHY.

Re-issue of

Pictorial Geography, for the Instruction of Young Children. Price 1s. 6d.; mounted on rollers 3s. 6d.

Gaultier's Familiar Geography. With a concise Treatise on the Artificial Sphere, and two coloured Maps, illustrative of the principal Geographical Terms. 16mo, 3s. cloth.

Butler's Outline Maps, and Key, or GEOGRAPHICAL AND BIOGRAPHICAL EXERCISES; with a Set of Coloured Outline Maps, designed for the use of Young Persons. By the late WILLIAM BUTLER. Enlarged by the Author's Son, J. O. BUTLER. Thirty-sixth Edition. Revised 4s.

Tabular Views of the Geography and Sacred History of Palestine, AND OF THE TRAVELS OF ST. PAUL. By A. T. WHITE. Price 1s. sewed.

GRAMMAR, &c.

A Compendious Grammar, AND PHILOLOGICAL HAND-BOOK OF THE ENGLISH LANGUAGE, for the use of Schools and Candidates for the Army and Civil Service Examinations. By J. G. COLQUHOUN, Esq., Barrister-at-Law. Fcap. 8vo. Cloth 2s. 6d.

Darnell, G. Grammar made Intelligible to Children. Being a Series of short and simple Rules, with ample Explanations of Every Difficulty, and copious Exercises for Parsing; in Language adapted to the comprehension of very Young Students. New and Revised Edition. Cloth, 1s.

Darnell, G. Introduction to English Grammar. Price 3d. Being the first 32 pages of "Grammar made Intelligible."

GRAMMAR—*continued.*

Darnell, T. Parsing Simplified: an Introduction and Companion to all Grammars; consisting of Short and Easy Rules, with Parsing Lessons to each. Price 1*s.* cloth.

Lovechilds, Mrs. The Child's Grammar. 50th Edition. 9*d.* cloth.

A Word to the Wise, or HINTS ON THE CURRENT IMPROPRIETIES OF EXPRESSION IN WRITING AND SPEAKING. By PARRY GWYNNE. Sixteenth Thousand. 18mo, price 6*d.* sewed; or 1*s.* cloth, gilt edges.

Harry Hawkins's H-Book; showing how he learned to aspirate his H's. Eighth Thousand. Sewed, price 6*d.*

Prince of Wales's Primer (The). With 340 Illustrations by J. GILBERT. Price 6*d.*

Darnell, G. Short and Certain Road to Reading. Being a Series EASY LESSONS in which the Alphabet is so divided as to enable the Child to read many pages of Familiar Phrases before he has learned half the letters. Cloth, 6*d.*; or in Four parts, paper covers, 1½*d.* each.

Sheet Lessons Being Extracts from the above, printed in very large, bold type. Price, for the Set of Six Sheets, 6d.; or, neatly mounted on boards, 3*s.*

ARITHMETIC AND ALGEBRA.

Darnell, G. Arithmetic made Intelligible to Children. Being a Series of GRADUALLY ADVANCING EXERCISES, intended to employ the Reason rather than the Memory of the Pupil; with ample Explanations of Every Difficulty, in Language adapted to the comprehension of very young Students. Cloth, 1*s.* 6*d.*

*** This work may be had in Three parts—Part I., price 6*d.* Part II., price 9*d.* Part III., price 6*d.* A KEY to Parts II and III., price 1*s.* (Part I. does not require a Key.)

Cayzer, T. S. One Thousand Arithmetical Tests, or THE EXAMINER'S ASSISTANT Specially adapted, by a novel arrangement of the subject, for Examination Purposes, but also suited for general use in Schools. With a complete set of Examples and Models of Work. Price 1*s.* 6*d.*

Key with Solutions of all the Examples in the One Thousand Arithmetical Tests. Price 4*s.* 6*d.* cloth. The Answers only, price 1s. 6d. cloth.

One Thousand Algebraical Tests; on the same plan. 8vo, price 2*s.* 6*d.* cloth.

ANSWERS to the Algebraical Tests, price 2*s.* 6*d.* cloth.

PUBLISHED BY GRIFFITH AND FARRAN. 31

ARITHMETIC, &c.—*continued.*
Theory and Practice of the Metric System of Weights and Measures. By Prof. LEONE LEVI, F.S.A., F.S.S. Sewed 1s.
Essentials of Geometry, Plane and Solid (The), as taught in Germany and France. By J. R. MORELL. Numerous Diagrams. 2s., cloth.

Artizan Cookery and How to Teach it. By a Pupil of the National Training School for Cookery, South Kensington. Sewed, price 6d.

NEEDLEWORK.
By the Examiner of Needlework to the School Board for London.

NEEDLEWORK DEMONSTRATION SHEETS
Exhibit, by Diagrams and Descriptions, the formation of Stitches in Elementary Needlework. The size of the Sheets is 30 × 22 inches. Price, 9d. each; or, mounted on rollers and varnished, 2s. 6d.

Whip Stitch for Frills, and Fern or Coral Stitch ... 1 Sheet	Grafting Stocking Material...	1 Sheet
Hemming, Seaming, and Stitching ... ... 1 ,,	Stocking Web Stitch	1 ,,
Button Hole ... ... 1 ,,	True Marking Stitch	1 ,,
Fisherman's Stitch for Braiding Nets ... ... 1 ,,	Alphabets for Marking ...	6 ,,
Herring Bone ... ... 1 ,,	Setting in Gathers or "Stocking" Knotting or Seeding (English Method)	1 ,,

The Demonstration Frame for Class Teaching, with Special Needle and Cord. Price complete, 7s. 6d.

Plain Needlework arranged in Six Standards, with Hints for the Management of Classes, and Appendix on Simultaneous Teaching. Eighteenth Thousand. Price 6d.

Plain Knitting and Mending arranged in Six Standards, with 20 Diagrams. Eleventh Thousand. Price 6d.

Plain Cutting Out for Standards IV., V., and VI., as now required by the Government Educational Department. Adapted to the principles of Elementary Geometry. Fifth Thousand. Price 1s.

A set of the Diagrams referred to in the book may be had separately, printed on stout paper and enclosed in an envelope. Price 1s.

*** *These works are recommended in the published Code of the Educational Department.*

Needlework, Schedule III. Exemplified and Illustrated. Intended for the use of Young Teachers and of the Upper Standards in Elementary Schools. By Mrs. E. A. CURTIS, a former Head Mistress of the Home and Colonial Training School. Cloth limp, with 30 Illustrations, price 1s.

DARNELL'S COPY-BOOKS

FOR BOARD, PRIVATE, & PUBLIC SCHOOLS.
Adapted to the Grades of the New Educational Code.

DARNELL'S LARGE POST COPY-BOOKS,
16 Nos., 6d. each.

The first ten of which have, on every alternate line, appropriate and carefully-written copies in Pencil-coloured Ink, to be first written over and then imitated, the remaining numbers having Black Head-lines for imitation only, THE WHOLE GRADUALLY ADVANCING FROM A SIMPLE STROKE TO A SUPERIOR SMALL HAND.

No.
1. Elementary (Strokes, &c.)
2. Single Letters.
3, 4. Large Text (Short Words).
5. Text, Large Text, and Figures.
6. Round Text, Capitals, and Figures.
7. Text, Round and Small.

No.
8, 9, 10. Text, Round, Small, and Figures.
11, 12. Round, Small, and Figures.
13, 14. Round and Small.
15, 16. Small Hand.

DARNELL'S FOOLSCAP COPY-BOOKS,
24 Nos., oblong, 3d. each, on the same plan; or, Superior Paper, Marble Covers, 4d. each.

No.
1. Elementary (Strokes, &c.)
2. Single Letters.
3, 4. Large Text (Short Words).
5. Text, Large Text, and Figures.
6. Text, Round, and Capitals.
7. Round, Small, and Figures.
8. Text, Round, and Figures.

No.
9. Round, Small, and Figures.
10, 11. Round and Small.
12, 13, 15. Round, Small, and Figures.
14. Round and Small.
16 to 20. Small Hand.
21. Ornamental Hands.
22 to 24. Ladies' Angular Writing.

DARNELL'S UNIVERSAL COPY-BOOKS,
16 Nos., 2d. each, on the same plan.
N.B.—Contents same as " Post Copy-Books."

ELEMENTARY FRENCH AND GERMAN WORKS.

Le Babillard: an Amusing Introduction to the French Language. By a FRENCH LADY Ninth Edition. 16 Plates. 2s. cloth.

Les Jeunes Narrateurs, ou PETITS CONTES MORAUX. With a Key to the difficult Words and Phrases. 3rd Edition. 2s. cloth.

Pictorial French Grammar (The). For the use of Children. By MARIN DE LA VOYE With 80 Illus. Royal 16mo, 1s. 6d. cloth.

Rowbotham's New and Easy Method of Learning the French Genders. New Edition. 6d.

Bellenger's French Word and Phrase Book; containing a select Vocabulary and Dialogues. New Edition. Price 1s.

Der Schwätzer, or THE PRATTLER. An Amusing Introduction to the German Language. Sixteen Illustrations. Price 2s. cloth.

GRIFFITH AND FARRAN, LONDON.

www.ingramcontent.com/pod-product-compliance
Lightning Source LLC
Chambersburg PA
CBHW022044230426
43672CB00008B/1061